Human Geography in Eastern Europe and the Former Soviet Union

Human Geography in Eastern Europe and the Former Soviet Union

Ludwik Mazurkiewicz
Polish Academy of Sciences

With a Foreword by
R. J. Johnston
University of Essex

Belhaven Press
London

Halsted Press
an imprint of John Wiley & Sons, Inc.
New York   Toronto

© L. Mazurkiewicz 1992

First published in Great Britain in 1992 by
Belhaven Press (a division of Pinter Publishers Limited)
25 Floral Street, London WC2E 9DS

British Library Cataloguing in Publication Data
A CIP catalogue record for this book is available from the British Library.

ISBN 1 85293 175 2

Co-published in the Americas by
Halsted Press, an imprint of John Wiley & Sons, Inc. New York Toronto
605 Third Ave, New York, NY 10158-0012

Library of Congress Cataloging-in-Publication Data available

ISBN 0470-21905-X

Typeset by BookEns Ltd, Baldock, Herts.
Printed and bound in Great Britain by
Biddles Ltd, Guildford and King's Lynn

Contents

Foreword

The development of an academic discipline such as geography reflects the interaction of three sets of factors: the trend of ideas; the individuals concerned with those ideas; and the environment within which they work. The relative importance of the three varies over time and space, as this book makes very clear.

To purists, progress within a discipline follows a 'natural course': one set of research findings points to the next set of questions, so that the scientists are carried along by the trend of ideas and nothing else. Many doubt whether such purity is attainable, however, and few would claim that it has been achieved. The conduct of science is normally determined by scientists, working both individually and together. Individuals decide what it is that interests them within a discipline, and structure their research activities accordingly – although funding agencies may determine whether they can afford that which they propose. As they work, the scientists take account of what some others are doing, ignore the work of a second group, and perhaps even distort the findings of a third. As Kuhn makes clear in his classic work on *The Structure of Scientific Revolutions*, understanding developments in a discipline requires appreciation of the psychology of the individuals involved and the sociology of the communities to which they belong. Without that appreciation, the history of a discipline cannot be understood, because what is done, by whom, and why reflects their individual perceptions of scientific priorities.

Those perceptions are coloured by the environment in which the scientists operate, both their working environment (their university department or institute laboratory, for example) and their socio-political environment (the condition of the national economy, for example, and the goals of those in charge of the state apparatus). The latter may be a very strong influence, both directly and indirectly. Scientists may individually and collectively take cues from the environment as to how they should orient their work, and behave accordingly, or they may be directed to favour certain types of work over others – through either dictat or the discriminatory channelling of funds.

Geographers in the market economies of the English-speaking world generally believe that – apart from the mobilization of intellectual resources during wartime, and especially during the Second World War – there has been very little direct influence by the state apparatus on the conduct of their discipline. There can be little doubt that geography has been expected to serve the general needs of the political economy, and that during periods of recession this perceived requirement has been enhanced. But rarely, if ever, have either state or academic politicians made clear pronouncements that geographers must do certain things and not expend resources, including their own time, on others, although the priorities adopted by funding bodies (most of them state-sponsored) have pressed researchers in certain directions and some scholars have strongly promoted a certain orientation.

This has certainly not been the case in the command economies that characterized the USSR from 1917 to 1991 and Eastern Europe for the shorter period 1945–1990. There, as Ludwik Mazurkiewicz's account makes clear, certain types of work were proscribed – including the study of society-environment interrelationships – because their content was inconsistent with the state ideology. The discipline was very substantially stunted, with only two major themes during the 1940s and 1950s in the USSR according to Mazurkiewicz – the study of territorial production complexes and of socio-cultural territorial complexes. Prior to the October Revolution, the discipline had developed in Russia along similar lines to its progress in other countries: and since the liberalization of academia in the 1980s, the same situation has again commenced.

The lasting intellectual impact of that seventy-year period can only be evaluated with the greater hindsight that at present we cannot possess. For the present, all we can do is gain an appreciation of what was and was not allowed to geographers during that period. This is what the present book does, fulfilling an urgent need for English readers. In preparing it, Dr Mazurkiewicz illuminates the problems inherent to such societies, and aids our reflections on the growing politicization of academia within the rampant market economies of the English-speaking world at present – to which those escaping the heavy hand of totalitarianism are currently attracted.

In 1973, Bill Bunge ended a well-known essay by asking if the world could be full of happy regions: in reflecting on the history of geography in Anglo-America and in the Soviet empire during the last half-century, I am led to wonder whether there can be a happy medium between totalitarian determination of a discipline's academic content on the one hand and its total subjection to the market place on the other. That is what I hope we can all aspire to.

R. J. JOHNSTON
Vice-Chancellor
University of Essex

Preface

The aim of the book is to outline and explain the study of human geography in Eastern Europe and the Soviet Union. The focus is on ideas, concepts and approaches that have emerged during the last one hundred years and which have successively shaped the content and nature of the discipline. Particular attention is paid to recent decades and current changes as well as possible future developments in the light of profound contemporary transformations in the social and economic life of the region.

The idea of the book and its structure is to a considerable degree similar to that of R. J. Johnston's *Geography and geographers*. There are two main reasons for using the latter as a general model. First, Johnston's book has so far been the only work to present clearly and convincingly how to write about the nature of the geographical discipline with reference to a particular region. Second, the segmentation of the history of the discipline proposed by Johnston is similar to that recognized in East European and Soviet human geography. This is the result of enduring western, mainly Anglo-American influence which meant that the way in which the discipline developed in the East European–Soviet region resembles to a large degree the evolution of Anglo-American human geography.

As in Johnston's work, the history of human geography is understood in this volume as a reconstruction of ideas and concepts concerning the nature of the discipline. They have been invented, or adapted, by particular scholars whose contribution to the process of the discipline's development has been crucial. In other words, the concern here is to present geography as other (outstanding) geographers see it, or have seen it in the past. Attention is paid to the major results of the activity of these individuals, as well as the circumstances in which they worked and produced their output.

Their activity and output have been conditioned by certain general rules which have governed the development of science. These rules are described in the literature by appropriate models of scientific progress. Following the point of view proposed by Johnston, a paradigm model of the evolution of the academic discipline is adopted. Some basic assumptions of the model are modified according to the propositions that appeared in the literature after Johnston's work was published. Nevertheless, the main idea offered in this work remains the same. This is the idea that the process of the discipline's development consists of different periods of scientific thought, or world view, emerging in succession and presenting distinct content in terms of what the discipline studies, how and why. Such an approach is applied in this book with reference to the history of human geography in Eastern Europe and the former USSR.

Not all aspects of the general structure of Johnston's work are followed in this volume. There are some major differences between the two. First of all, there is no division into the outer and the inner volume. Theoretical and methodological considerations concerning human geography in terms of the models developed within the history of science are reduced to the dimension which is necessary to understand the argument. They are placed in the first, introductory chapter. Accordingly, the last chapter presents the most likely scenario of the development of the discipline in the immediate future.

While Johnston's work is an account of the last four decades of the development of disciplinary knowledge in the Anglo-American region, the history of East European and Soviet human geography outlined in this volume is traced back far earlier, to the beginnings of the modern period which started in the region in the late nineteenth century. This is dictated not only by the need to obtain a more complete and thereby comprehensive picture of the history, but primarily to shed more light on past events, particularly those which occurred in the pre-socialist era and which are hardly known to present-day readers in the West.

Theories and concepts that appeared in the region have come from three major sources. Firstly, they have been created within particular national geographies. Secondly, there was an impact from Soviet ideas mainly after the last war, and thirdly, there has been the almost permanent influence of western geography which decisively shaped the character and form of the discipline. While the first source has tended towards the diversification of the content and nature of human geography in various countries, the other two sources have acted as a unifying factor. Since they have predominated during its history, the discipline has developed in a very similar way in certain parts of the region. What is more, in the space of more than four decades this process has occurred in almost identical political, social and economic circumstances, which has constituted an additional factor in levelling out the differences among countries. As a result, human geography in the region has presented a high degree of homogeneity arising from the similarity of the nature and content of particular national research fields. For this reason, the history of the discipline is not systematized territorially here. As there are no substantial differences among the countries in the region in terms of the way in which human geography has been pursued, the problem of the reconstruction of the history of the discipline resolves itself into the basic questions of how and why the ideas and concepts originated in time. The question 'where' is of somewhat less importance and plays a complementary role with reference to the time analysis. Particular countries are considered to the degree which is proportional to their contribution to the overall process of disciplinary development.

The literature on the history of East European–Soviet human geography is very differentiated. English literature is insignificant. Outside it there is material written in native languages. This varies in its quantity from one country to another. The largest is the Soviet literature. Other countries have a somewhat modest output. All this is fragmentary, however, dispersed among various sources and published accidentally rather than according to any deliberate, purposeful scheme. In addition, this literature mainly concerns the history of human geography in particular countries and there is still a lack of work which systematizes the problem and provides any synthesis from the point of view of the region as a whole. The present volume is intended to fill the gap.

Seven countries are distinguished in the book to constitute the region: Bulgaria, Czechoslovakia, Hungary, Poland, Romania, Yugoslavia and the former USSR. Literature from these countries has made it possible to present the history of the discipline within the region since the last decades of the nineteenth century. Two countries are excluded from the analysis: the GDR and Albania. The literature on the history of the discipline in the former encompasses the three last decades only, and there is practically no material available with reference to the latter.

As the present book is intended to describe the history of human geography in the region, its organization reflects the segmentation (periodization) of this history. The discussion of how the book is organized is preceded by the identification of major periods or stages within the process of the discipline's development. They are distinguished in the first chapter, 'Introduction'.

1

Introduction

The main purpose of this chapter is to identify major periods or stages within the history of human geography in Eastern Europe and the former USSR. Before this question is answered, however, the problem of how academic life is organized in the region is discussed, as there are some differences from the Anglo-American world. This problem is presented briefly in the first part of the chapter. In the second part, periods in the process of disciplinary development are identified as the basis of the structure of the book. Its organization is outlined at the end of the chapter.

The organization of academic life in human geography in Eastern Europe and the former USSR

The organization of academic life in contemporary East European and Soviet human geography has been the result of the merging of two models of research activity: the university model, with traditions going back to the latter part of the nineteenth century, and the model elaborated in the USSR before the last war, based on the institution of the Academy of Sciences. The latter was introduced in East European human geography in the 1950s and since then, in every country of the region, human geography has been pursued in a characteristic, parallel way resting on the above two models. The institution of the Academy of Sciences has played a key role in the organization and co-ordination of research activity in the field. This role has resulted immediately from the planned character of socio-economic life in all countries in the region. Since the beginnings of the 1960s, research projects have been co-ordinated within the framework of the five-year national socio-economic plans, and the Academies of Sciences in particular countries have been responsible for accomplishing research aspects of these plans.

Institutes of Geography in Academies of Sciences do not teach students. This task is performed by departments of geography in universities which, aside from teaching, contribute to the research projects supervised and guided by the Institutes. At the same time, both systems provide a very similar model of organization of academic life based on practically the same career structure. In the two systems, this structure consists of a few parallel stages which represent the same levels of the professional career ladder, and it is quite common to cross, at a similar level, from one system to the other. This organization is very common in all countries of the region, and local differences, if they exist, are insignificant compared to the essential features of the model.

In order to become a member of the academic community an individual must show the personal qualities necessary in academic work as a post-graduate student. These qualities may be recognized by the supervisor in the course of undergraduate training, and then such a person after post-graduate work is engaged as a member of university staff, or obtains appropriate recommendations when applying for a job in another university, or the Institute of Geography in the Academy of Sciences. As a rule, individuals trying to enter the world of academic geography have been postgraduates in geography. There is, however, quite a large number of representatives of other disciplines, primarily from the social sciences.

There is another way to become a member of academic society. This is through the institution of postgraduate training which is organized in each country both by universities and the Institute of Geography of the Academy of Sciences. In principle a candidate (an applicant) must pass an examination which is another method of checking his or her qualities from the viewpoint of future research work.

Regardless of which way is chosen, the aim of undertaking a research career is to obtain academic degrees. The way via the institution of post-graduate training is faster. It does not assume involvement in teaching even if an individual is a member of the university's department staff. Postgraduate training takes the form of a few years' (usually three or four) basic course, during which some instruction is provided based on a uniform curriculum, the remaining time being spent on individual work and the preparation of the doctoral dissertation. A postgraduate who is a member of the academic teaching staff, on the other hand, is obliged to teach and complete his or her research degree at the same time. A limited-tenure teaching post is given to such an individual for one year or a little more, to complete the doctoral thesis.

When completed, the dissertation is criticized in writing by at least two examiners and the candidate is called upon to defend the topic at an open public debate in front of an examining body. In order to be admitted to the public defence, the candidate needs to pass a doctoral examination which consists usually of three topics: geography, a foreign language, and philosophy or political economy. When successful, the individual obtains his or her academic degree, which in most countries of the region is termed a 'candidate of science' and corresponds with the Doctor of Philosophy degree in the Anglo-American world.

There is another, higher scientific degree unknown in the Anglo-American tradition which is in use within the academic system in East European countries and the former USSR. This is the degree of doctor of sciences that presents the final step in an academic career and whose accomplishment leads directly to a professorship. The degree can be obtained by a person holding the degree of candidate of sciences. To apply for the doctor of sciences degree a candidate must submit another dissertation. This dissertation is then discussed and defended in front of an examining body. This defence is not public, but takes place during the session of the scientific council of a department or Institute of Geography of the Academy of Sciences. The discussion and defence is based on criticism written by at least three opponents.

There are three professional academic titles in the discipline throughout the region, with which three levels of the academic career ladder correspond. These are dozent, professor and full professor. The first post is comparable with that of associate professor in the American model or reader in the British model. In most countries the title 'dozent' is used in universities only, whereas in the Academy of Sciences the term 'doctor of science' is applied.

Movement from one category to another is promotional and occurs on the basis of recognition of academic excellence. Each category has its own salary scale and with each is connected a position in academic leadership. Scholars holding the above posts are as a rule appointed to guide activity within the three main areas of academic life – research, teaching and administration. The highest professional grade is a full professorship which gives the opportunity to perform major functions to control activity within all three fields. The position of professor and dozent differ little, however, from that of full professor in terms of the tasks in managing academic life. In practice, professors and dozents may be appointed to the major posts as well to provide academic leadership.

Major stages in the development of the discipline and the organization of the book

In this section, the organization of the book is discussed. As the book is about the history of human geography in Eastern Europe and the former

Soviet Union, its organization should first of all reflect the major periods or stages of disciplinary development in the region. Their identification is therefore the starting point of the discussion here. The discussion has certain methodological aspects. They are outlined, however, only to the extent necessary to understand the argument presented both in this chapter and later in the book. The structure of the disciplinary history will serve as a basis for organizing the content of the book. This organization is presented at the end of the chapter.

There is, in general, a lack of studies of how the history of the discipline in the region is structured. Some investigations have been conducted in a few countries, but they are confined to a national scale. In the absence of appropriate sources, the discussion here is of necessity introductory and needs some methodological background. This is related to two basic assumptions applied in Johnston's book. The first assumption is that the criterion for distinguishing periods within the history of human geography is the dominant paradigm, or the way in which problems identified within the theoretical framework of the discipline are solved by the majority of researchers. The second assumption concerns how the paradigmatic structure of the discipline evolves, that is, how the paradigm currently predominating is replaced by a new philosophy. There are, according to Johnston, two kinds of factors conditioning paradigmatic evolution: external factors related to the social, economic and political environment in which the discipline is embedded, and factors internal to the discipline (Johnston 1983).

The external environment is a major influence on the content of human geography. Changes within this environment stimulate changes in research practice which, in turn, lead to the creation of new orientations that gradually supersede earlier approaches. These changes occur within the discipline. The way this takes place is described with reference to the so-called paradigm shift model. It assumes that the hitherto existing obsolete orientation is replaced by new paradigm(s) giving better responses to the questions that the former approaches have failed to answer. The process of disciplinary evolution consists in a series of paradigms which follow in succession in time.

The point of view adopted here includes a modification of the above internal mechanism of reproduction of the conceptual content of the discipline. The mechanism proposed here is described by the approach known in the literature as evolutionary theory (Eyles 1984). What distinguishes this theory from the paradigm shift model is the stress placed on the significance of earlier ideas and concepts. New paradigms that appear do not replace the older approaches. The latter survive, acquiring what Eyles calls 'relict forms', and maintain their role. The newly-emerging paradigms thus overlap those already existing and the body of disciplinary knowledge is created in a cumulative way. Paradigms coexist, modifying their structure and changing their significance with time under the impact of both earlier orientations and those which are newly appearing. 'Evolutionary theory [. . .] with its reference to relicts, the problematic path of development and the coexistence of competing systems links the history of ideas firmly with social change. Such a view does not suggest that earlier ideas are relict in any pejorative sense but that they maintain a significant role even when others come to the fore' (Eyles 1984, 248).

The evolutionary approach better describes the mechanism of changes within the process of development of human geography in the East European–Soviet region. It is possible to explain in these terms not only the branching of disciplinary knowledge through the addition of new orientations, but also the revival of earlier concepts and ideas which survive in a relict form.

The above approach, underpinned by the assumption that the external environment has a decisive influence on the content of the discipline, allows us to distinguish five major periods within the last hundred years of the history of human geography in the region. These periods are characterized briefly below as they form the basis of the structure of the book.

The first period covers the last decades of the nineteenth century and the years before the socialist political system emerged in the region. The beginning of the stage was marked by the establishment of geography in the universities; this became the starting point in providing a specialist training in the subject, forming the necessary paradigmatic framework for the pursuit of the discipline. Following the literature, this is termed the modern period. In Russia, it included some developments in earlier decades which did not differ much in their character from what was the nature of modern geography there. The rich output of Russian geography in the years preceding the modern period meant that the discipline presented a high level of development until the end of this period. In Eastern Europe geography developed later, relying primarily on ideas and theories adopted from western schools. Some differences between both geographies caused by the somewhat distinct evolution of geography in Russia are the reason that, as well as 'modern', the term 'pre-socialist' is used here. In this period, three major paradigms developed within human geography in the region. These were: exploration; environmental determinism and possibilism, and the regional approach. This was one of the richest stages in the history of the discipline in terms of the quantity and diversity of the orientations.

The second phase in the process of development of human geography in the region coincided with the imposition of Stalinism in the East European subregion. Within the field it was marked by a somewhat strained adaptation of the Soviet model of economic geography. This focused on the problem of region and regionalization as applied primarily to the sphere of material production. Dealing with economic phenomena, it found its expression in creating interest in topical geography mostly in economic activities in order to explain particular regional outcomes. Topical specialism started to develop only by the end of the 1950s, however, and that was why regional studies presented the most characteristic way of pursuing human geography at that time. A regional paradigm was developed, within which a number of theories of economic region were invented, some presenting opposing points of view. The phase ended towards the end of the 1950s when the first western ideas began to penetrate the discipline in the region. This was the consequence of the partial liberalization of social and political life connected with the liquidation of the most severe attributes of Stalinism.

The third period started at the beginning of the 1960s. It was characterized by a wide adoption of a western, positivist paradigm, particularly in Eastern Europe. In the USSR, production-oriented economic geography was gradually enriched with human and social aspects. In both parts of the region new paradigms were applied in two forms: spatial science studies and the systems approach. The former studies tended to explain observed territorial patterns in terms of the influence of space, especially distance, on human behaviour. Compared with them, the systems approach met with less interest, mainly because of greater theoretical complexity and the demand for a more compound empirical material. The period came to an end at the end of the 1970s when signs of approaching crisis became clearly perceptible.

The fourth phase in the process of human geography development started at the beginning of the 1980s when social and political crisis swept gradually over the countries of the region. Disappointment with the inability of the positivist, economically-oriented paradigm to deal with relevant social problems created a search for new approaches. As a result, a humanist and radical geography appeared largely under the influence of the western schools. This was complemented by some positivist models adopted to examine social phenomena in space, and by behavioural studies focusing on these phenomena at the level of particular human individuals. All this led to the creation of social geography, the development of which became the most characteristic feature of the period.

The beginnings of the fifth stage are marked by deep political and social changes in the region at the end of the 1980s. New social and economic problems are emerging and, combined with those that appeared in the previous period, are likely to last until the end of this decade. They constitute new subject matter for human geography and pose new research problems/questions.

The organization of the volume reflects this periodization of the history of the discipline. Each chapter discusses one successive period from this sequence. The final chapter offers conclusions which concern the most likely developments within the discipline by the end of the 1990s in the light of profound contemporary transformations in the social and economic life of the region.

2
Geography in pre-socialist Eastern Europe and Russia

In this book, the history of the discipline in the region is analysed starting from the modern period. The term 'modern' is used after James and Martin (1981). They defined it as the stage within the history of geography that began with the introduction of the discipline into the universities, and ended with the outbreak of the Second World War. Before that time, in the so-called classical period, geographical studies were undertaken largely by scholars trained in other fields. When geography was established in the universities the appropriate conditions emerged for a specialist training in the subject. These conditions comprised: a paradigm, or model of pursuing the research work in the field; departments of geography offering advanced training within the paradigm, and paid jobs for providing this training. When these conditions were satisfied, geography started to develop as a professional academic discipline (James and Martin 1981).

Conditions such as these emerged in the region in the last three decades of the nineteenth century. There were some particular circumstances, however, that created a distinction in the way in which geography developed in Eastern Europe and Russia. These were the pre-modern, or classical traditions of geographical studies. In Eastern Europe such traditions hardly existed and the discipline started to develop as a professional field by applying the paradigms which were adopted from modern western schools. At the same time, geography in Russia had already been pursued for a long time in a well-organized, semi-professional way. This was the main reason that, at the start of the modern period, the discipline relied entirely on its own concepts and methodology elaborated during the preceding decades.

The modern period, according to James and Martin, ended in 1945. In the East European–Soviet region, however, it is assumed that the end of the

Second World War was not as important a demarcation point in the history of the discipline as was another event. This was the emergence of a new, socialist system which changed profoundly all aspects of political, social and economic life including academic activity. If taken into account, this criterion means that the end of the modern period is dated differently in each part of the region. It lasted in Eastern Europe until the last world war, whereas in Russia it came to an end much earlier with the outbreak of the Bolshevik Revolution in 1917. This distinction, and the differences concerning the traditions of the pre-modern history of the discipline in the two subregions, are the main reasons that the modern period is discussed here separately. The chapter is thus divided into two parts. In the first part, geography in Russia is discussed not only in the modern phase, but also in the decades preceding the modern, as both time intervals are closely connected and constitute one period rather than two separate stages. The modern period in East European geography is outlined in the second part.

Since there are important differences in the history of the modern era in the two subregions, the term 'modern' is replaced by the label 'pre-socialist' or 'pre-revolutionary' as in the title of this chapter.

Pre-revolutionary geography in Russia

The modern phase in the history of the discipline in Russia lasted only thirty-three years from the establishment of the first chair of geography in the country in 1884 at Moscow University to the outbreak of the Bolshevik Revolution in 1917. This short time meant that what happened to geography then was a continuation of its evolution in the preceding decades, rather than the result of autonomous development during the thirty-year period. 160 years before the modern period began in the 1880s, another important event in the history of the discipline took place. This was the establishment of the St Petersburg Academy of Sciences in 1724, which was the first institution in the world to co-ordinate geographical studies (Gerasimov 1976, 33). As a result, the discipline started to be pursued in a new, more organized way, which was in firm contrast to earlier activity within the field. This continued until the modern period began when the discipline obtained a new, professional form. This did not change the character of the research approach, however, which was elaborated during the decades that passed. Geographical studies within the modern period inherited so much from the previous 160 years that it is more justifiable to speak about one continuous process of disciplinary development that lasted until 1917, rather than about two separate periods (classical and modern) which differed in their academic output. This nearly two-centuries-long process is defined here as a pre-revolutionary geography in Russia. This is discussed in terms of the most significant events that shaped its nature during the long process of evolution. The events are presented in relation to four distinct paradigms which operated within the discipline at that time. These were the same orientations that were typical then of geography in other parts of the world, i.e. exploration, the regional approach, environmental determinism and possibilism. The paradigms are presented in three sections (environmental determinism and possibilism are discussed together) into which the text below is divided.

Exploration

Exploration as an activity to gain information about particular parts of the country began relatively early in Russia. This was largely the consequence of the policy of the contemporary rulers who strived to convert their country into a modern world power. They realized that such a conversion required profound political and economic reforms; these, especially the latter, were impossible without prior recognition of the economic potential contained within the vast territory of the country. That was largely why, during the reign of Peter the Great and his immediate successors, geography developed more rapidly than other disciplines (Gerasimov 1978, 31). The aim of geographical studies was to provide information about the distribution of the country's huge natural resources. Yet such an activity required a systematic exploration of its territory. In order to plan and co-ordinate exploration on a large scale, the St Petersburg Academy of Sciences was founded in 1724 'as a main centre for resolving the most important geographical problems' (Gerasimov 1976, 32). In the first decades, the Academy was staffed mainly by scholars from Western Europe to secure as rapid progress as possible. Most of these scholars were Germans who were responsible for organization and sending expeditions to various parts of the country. Many of them contributed much to put the vast territory of the imperium on the map. The most famous were K. Bering, X. Pallas, I. Gmellin, Y. Steller, G. Miller and I. German (Gerasimov 1976).

With time, the exploratory activity acquired gradually the attributes of a purposeful academic undertaking. Expeditions had as their objective to survey the natural environment of diverse parts of Russia, assess the advantages of their strategic location and accessibility to important communication routes, and identify places where useful natural resources were provided. This activity included not only new territories annexed by the Russian Empire during its rapid eastward expansion, but also other parts of Russia known and recognized earlier, for example, the northern part of European Russia.

Statistical and cartographical material which gradually accumulated was classified and used for describing the territory of the country. The first description of Russia was made by I. K. Kirilov in his work of 1727 entitled *The flourishing conditions of the all Russia state*, 'which presented information on population, industry, trade and transportation by *gubernyas* (large administrative units), provinces and cities. Some of the material was presented in the form of tables, which was unusual at the time' (Nikitin 1966, 4). A few years later, Kirilov completed his work with the first atlas of Russia (Gerasimov 1976).

Kirilov's work stimulated further efforts to describe more accurately different parts of the national territory. To this end the first land-surveying project was elaborated by V. N. Tatishchev who wanted to cover the whole of Russia by cartographic and geodetic works. 'He sent geodesists to Siberia and European Russia to carry out this task. As a result, a number of maps were compiled which Tatishchev handed over to the Academy of Sciences' (Alexandrovskaya 1982, 130).

Gathering information and producing descriptions of the territory under survey soon became the most characteristic attribute of exploratory activity. Until the second half of the eighteenth century this activity was still unsystematized, however, consisting of many unco-ordinated efforts and not based on uniform methodology. The idea of organizing the exploratory paradigm around clearly-defined goals and unified methodology was proposed by M. V. Lomonosov, who was appointed in 1758 as the head of the world's first officially named department of geography (Gerasimov 1976, 65–73). He postulated that the expeditions should be sent with thoroughly and precisely defined lists of goals, and material should be gathered using uniform criteria. Lomonosov elaborated the lists of problems to be explored, trying to take account of all political, social and cultural aspects of the geography of the areas to which the expeditions were sent. His postulates were accomplished only after his death in 1765. By the end of the century the Academy had organized several geographical expeditions. They provided plenty of useful material which was not only used in producing systematic descriptions of particular parts of the country, but was also published in the form of various travel diaries and monographs (Alexandrovskaya 1982).

Apart from the Academy of Sciences, a significant role in promoting the exploration paradigm was played by various governmental bodies, among which was the well-known Free Economic Society. These organizations collected and published a large amount of geographical data dealing mainly with basic administrative-territorial units and cities (Nikitin 1966).

In the nineteenth century, and especially in its second half, exploration activity became more intensive in connection with the growth of capitalism in Russia and the related demand for the utilization of the rich resources of the national territory. New institutions emerged to promote further exploration of the country. Among them a leading role was played by the Russian Imperial Geographical Society founded in 1845. Departments of the Society focused mainly on physico-geographical specializations. There were two departments, however, which were concerned with human geography: the Department of Statistics, oriented primarily towards the problems of the economic life of the country as well as the life and social situation of the people, and the Department of Ethnography, dealing with the culture and way of life of the multinational Russian population (Nikitin 1966). The aim of the Society was 'the collection and dissemination in Russia of geographical information in general and about Russia in particular' (Nikitin 1966, 17). In practice, pursuing this goal consisted in supporting and sponsoring exploratory expeditions, popularizing geographical knowledge by organizing lecture meetings, and contributing to the works of other governmental bodies which were engaged mainly in statistical description of the country.

The Geographical Society's control over the form and character of exploration activity did not change in the modern period. The expeditions organized by the Society were sent primarily to yet-uncovered parts of the empire which, by the end of the nineteenth century, were the vast territories of the north part of the country adjoining the Arctic Ocean, and mountainous areas of eastern Siberia. There were also specialized expeditions sent to already known territories to explore certain aspects of their geography, for example, several expeditions were organized by the Department of Statistics and the Department of Ethnography (Nikitin 1966). Expeditions were also organized to undertake work outside Russia. Russian explorers were particularly active in the Pacific where many valuable discoveries were made, in particular in Melanesia. By the beginning of the 1920s all the territory of the country was explored, and expeditions were sent mainly to the Arctic Ocean. This area was later, during the Soviet period, a major focus of geographical exploration (Gerasimov 1976).

Educational activity provided by the Geographical Society was important in popularizing disciplinary knowledge and stimulating the interest of provincial geographers in the study of their areas. Meetings and lectures organized by the Society for the general public presented information about new discoveries and famous explorers. Research workers contributed at the same time by establishing the teaching of geography in universities.

Departments of the Society heard descriptions of various areas and cities presented by local people, and the best works were published in the Society publications which had a long tradition dating from the beginnings of the institution. This assisted other bodies in their efforts to collect and update statistical information about the country. The largest effort in this field was the first Russian population census in 1897 which was the only one in the pre-revolutionary period (Nikitin 1966).

Exploration as a specific kind of academic activity was intensely pursued during the classical and modern periods of pre-revolutionary Russian geography. Many geographers were engaged in this kind of work which, spanning almost 200 years, resulted in the gathering of rich information about the country as well as considerable scientific and travel literature. The relatively early beginnings of the exploratory paradigm in Russia, its intensive development, and large output of scientific material assembled over a long time were without doubt the primary factors stimulating the development of other paradigms which emerged even in the classical period. Many geographers who were involved in exploration applied at the same time the regional approach, and were interested in the problem of man's relation to his natural environment. The regional paradigm started to develop a little before the first debates on the man–nature relationship emerged, and so it is presented in the next section.

The regional paradigm

The concept of region began to be used when the first attempts to define geography were undertaken in Russia in the first half of the eighteenth century. Initially, the idea was formulated very broadly as a fundamental category of regional geography which, in turn, was considered an important part of geography as a whole. Such a point of view was adopted from western geographical thought, mainly from the theory presented by B. Varenius in his book, *General geography*. The book, published in 1650 in Amsterdam, was translated and edited in Russia in 1718 (Anuchin 1960, 32).

At the same time, the interest in the concept of region and regionalization among Russian geographers derived as perhaps nowhere else from practical needs. This was the time when expeditions were exploring large territories of the country and there was a firm demand for a suitable theoretical basis to interpret, generalize and use the large amount of information collected about new places.

The first to spread Varenius's ideas in Russia was V. N. Tatischev (Anuchin 1960, 34). Like Varenius, Tatishchev saw geography as the study of the earth's surface and its various fragments 'from large areas down to the scale of a town' (34). Regional geography, at the same time, was for him of great practical importance for the classification and interpretation of territorial data for governmental and economic (commercial) purposes. Geography of particular areas had to provide, according to him, a description of natural phenomena and conditions prevailing there, as well as characteristics of the population, its culture and social and economic aspects of life. Both physical and human aspects had to be divided, in turn, into separate topics and subjected to further analysis which was to be carried out in a historical manner indicating the origins of the phenomena as well as predicting their future destiny. The latter prescription was a consequence of the fact that Tatishchev was a historian and treated geography as a significant part of history. His geographical considerations he presented in one of the chapters of his main work, *The history of Russia* (Alexandrovskaya 1982). Tatishchev is regarded as the founder of geographical science in Russia. 'He saw the main task of geography as the regional description of the earth. This idea runs like a thread through all his creative works' (Alexandrovskaya 1982, 131). He first distinguished three basic aspects of regional analysis as physical, political (human) and historical description, emphasizing the necessity of examining phenomena in their spatial and time dimension to gain a full understanding of what occurs on the earth's surface (Anuchin 1960).

Tatishchev was the first who applied in practice his theoretical considerations on region and regionalization. He was the author of a regional description of Siberia, initiating and working out for the purposes of this work a questionnaire method used for the first time in Russia. He was also the first to propose the project of regionalization of the country using as a criterion the distribution of national minorities (Yoffa 1965).

Tatishchev's approach and ideas had a major influence on Lomonosov whose contribution to the development of geography in Russia is regarded as the largest among eighteenth-century scholars (Nikitin 1966). Lomonosov was an eminent, many-sided scholar widely known for his achievements in chemistry, physics and geology, who discovered among many things the atmosphere of Venus and the molecular character of matter (Alexandrovskaya 1982). In the middle of the century, Lomonosov became the head of the geography department in the Academy of Sciences, and from that time he devoted himself to developing the discipline. He shared Tatishchev's major assumptions regarding geography, and regional geography in particular. The latter was for him not only the description of places from the point of view of their environment, population and economy; he went further, and set forth the idea of analysing these components in their mutual interrelationships as the way to understand the differentiated character of the earth's surface. As Anuchin (1960, 35) holds, the problem of interdependence between man and the natural environment has been taken for granted since Lomonosov's era.

Much of Lomonosov's activity was oriented to practical aspects of geographical studies. He was not only one of the main persons responsible for sending out exploratory expeditions, but he was also immensely anxious to apply geographical knowledge to the process of the development of the national economy. According to Lomonosov, a proper way to accelerate this development was through the growth of industry, primarily metallurgy, as well as trade, both of which had conditions conducive to development in Russia thanks to its rich resources. Recognizing these resources and assessing the productive and economic potential of particular regions was to be the primary purpose of geography. Geography, for Lomonosov, should provide an accurate and detailed description of regions from the point of view of their natural conditions, the resources localized there and possibilities for their utilization, and the social and cultural characteristics of the population, including demographic information to predict future changes in the number of people living in particular places (Dick 1965). All these aspects were specified when expeditions were sent to gather information in a formal and comparable way. Everything possible had to be mapped or presented in the form of statistical data for future use by government as well as in the sphere of commercial development. Lomonosov himself did not undertake any regional analysis. His programmes for exploring various regions were applied as a useful methodological base to organize expeditions for a long time to come.

The first regional studies, providing many-sided analyses of particular areas of the national territory, emerged in the second half of the eighteenth century. Among them, two surveys presented a model form and gained international fame. These were S. P. Krashennikov's work on Kamchatka and P. I. Rychkov's regional study of the Orenburg *gubernya* (Nikitin 1966).

Krashennikov's work is often considered to be the first regional monograph in the world (Yugai 1985). Hooson (1968) indicates its similarity to the later output of A. Humboldt. The work was published in 1742. Because of its originality and scientific achievements it was greatly admired, and was translated into English in 1764 and French in 1767. Krashennikov was perhaps the first who applied Lomonosov's suggestion to analyse man and the natural environment in terms of their mutual interdependence. His book, a result of many years of field work, contained many examples of this relationship. It presented a very detailed and vivid description of the natural conditions of Kamchatka's environment, examining the relations between various phenomena, including volcanism and plant and animal life. In picturesque style the peculiarities of the social and cultural life of the population were shown, as well as details of the economic situation. Human life was described against the background of the rich natural environment, and many connections between man and his land were observed and analysed (Berg 1962).

Rychkov's work dealt with the vast territory of the Orenburg province that stretched then from the Urals to the deserts of Central Asia. In his study he used both factual material and maps from various periods of history which allowed him to present the historical development of the area under investigation. The description of the province concerned its natural conditions, its mineral resources, the population and its cultural and social characteristics, the economy, as well as the towns and their role in the development of the territory. The focus was not so much, as in Krashennikov's study, on the relations among particular phenomena, as on a reconstruction of how the natural features, population and economy of the region evolved over time. It was a new approach then, and the work attracted much interest, not only in Russia. Aside from the Russian edition in 1762, the book was published in Germany in 1772 (Yugai 1985).

Just at that time, the first attempts at regionalization appeared in Russian geography. In 1764, F. I. Soymov published the book in which he proposed the division of Siberia into six regions using economic characteristics. Each region was then divided into smaller units on the basis of the same criteria, and as a result the three-level regionalization of the area was arrived at (Lebedev 1952).

The first regional division of the country into natural units was proposed by A. F. Busching in 1766. He used the data he had collected concerning conditions of the physical environment. On this basis he divided the territory of the country into three major latitudinal belts characterized by different natural conditions (Nikitin 1966). The idea of Busching's regionalization has remained almost unchanged till the present day, and in fact still underlies contemporary physical regionalization of the country.

In the second decade of the nineteenth century the work entitled *Description of the statistics of the Russian state* was published by K. I. Arsenev. It was the first attempt to divide the country into regions using a broad collection of characteristics dealing with both natural conditions and the human life of the country. His regionalization constituted a spatial framework to describe the geography of the whole country. He distinguished ten major regions different from one another with respect to the assumed criteria, maintaining that the procedure of regionalization should use 'a few but tellingly characteristic traits' (Nikitin 1966, 14). In 1848, probably under the influence of Ogarev's new concept of region, Arsenev made amendments in his regional division, obtaining much improved results.

According to Nikitin (1966), in the period 1800–1861 fifteen various attempts appeared to divide the territory of Russia into regions. These attempts, as well as those applied before, were based on the concept of a region as a mental construct to classify things and phenomena distributed in space. In 1847 a different approach was proposed by N. P. Ogarev, who considered a region to be not a segment of the earth's surface, but a nodal, spatial structure distinguished from others by its economic specialization (Nikitin 1966). For Ogarev, regions were not spatial classes, the result of 'mind games' but really existing objects (Nikitin 1965). This was in accord with his conceptualization of geography as a category dealing only with real world phenomena. An example of one such phenomenon significant to the concept of the region were the so-called 'material forces of the economy' (Nikitin 1965, 318). Ogarev distinguished two major kinds of material forces, or economic activities. On the one hand, there were what he termed basic economic activities which occurred less frequently in space and constituted essential components of the productive structure of areas. These were specialized activities, the output of which was a measure by which particular areas shared in the global economy. Such output was the source of further development and richness of the places where the activities were localized. On the other hand, there were activities distributed more frequently in space and performing economic functions of a similar type. Their essential aim was to maintain basic economic activities in operation. Both kinds of activities, the basic and the auxiliary ones, were linked together by a network of functional relations constituting a regional structure whose core was the basic economic sector composed of one, or several specialized activities. This economic structure, together with the natural environment of the area and population living there, constituted a certain territorial and functional whole distinct from other such wholes by their economic specialization. Ogarev called these wholes economic regions (Nikitin 1965).

Ogarevs' ideas were far ahead of his time. What he invented may be called, in present terminology, elements of both nodal region and economic base theory. The degree of maturity of the Russian economy that time was not large, however, and presented too little heterogeneity of economic activities to verify the assumptions of the approach. Using these assumptions, Ogarev distinguished only a few regions in European Russia whose economic structure was advanced enough to identify specialized sectors (Nikitin 1965).

Ogarev's proposition about the political regionalization of Russia was interesting. Like many progressive intellectuals of that time, he believed that the only future for his homeland as a democratic country would be a federative system. He proposed to divide the future republican Russia into ten federal states, which he distinguished on the basis of ethnic and industrial principles (Nikitin 1965). Ogarev's model influenced and enriched the regional paradigm in Russia. Aside from the concept of the region as a uniform spatial class, another concept of region was used, based on the assumption of nodality and specialization.

The first to apply Ogarev's idea of region was Arsenev. Later, a few works appeared using as criteria the assumptions about region either as a nodal structure or as a function of economic specialization in space. An example of the first approach was the study of the grain trade carried out by a group of economists and geographers. They investigated sources of production, markets and centres of sale and, using assumptions of economic gravitation as well as analysing transport linkage, distinguished retail regions as areas centred around places supplying food (Nikitin 1966).

Economic specialization as a factor responsible for the formation of regions was probably best of all presented by A. I. Chuprov. In his work *The railroad economy* published in 1875–8, he analysed the influence of the rail transport network on commodity exchange and the location of production. Studying freight-flow characteristics, he was able to delimit railway regions with their main economic specializations (Nikitin 1965a).

The concept of the economic region and regionalization proposed by Ogarev was not, however, accepted by many geographers. In their opinion it was a one-sided, economic way of viewing the regional problem. Most geographers were more interested in a broader approach comprising both natural and human aspects of the problem. An older approach, therefore, based on the concept of the uniform region prevailed in geography at that time. This concept enabled geographers to combine various characteristics of the physical and human environment, and to look then for the order in their spatial arrangements.

In the second half of the nineteenth century, probably the most comprehensive regional analysis of the country was proposed by P. P. Semenov-Tyan-Shanski. He analysed the geographical distribution of the population in European Russia, and for the purposes of this analysis he proposed a system of regions which was initially based on natural criteria, and which later was enriched with social and economic characteristics (Saushkin 1965).

Semenov-Tyan-Shanski's work was the last important regional analysis in the classical period. In the next, modern period a few studies appeared concerning the problem of region and regionalization. In their form and character they did not differ from the model of the regional approach which was worked out in the preceding decades. The largest and most original contribution to the paradigm were studies by V. P. Semenov-Tyan-Shanski, the son of P. P. Semenov-Tyan-Shanski. He was the editor of the largest work on regionalization that appeared in Russian geography. This multi-volume work was entitled *Trade and industry of European Russia by regions*, and was published in 1906–11. European Russia was divided into twelve latitudinal belts, each composed of a number of microregions. 1,065 such units were distinguished, comprising a system which was independent of administrative divisions. Every microregion was described in detail from the point of view of natural conditions, population and its various features, as well as economic life and its essential characteristics. The work included a map showing the distribution of industry, agriculture and trade by belts and microregions (Valskaya 1965).

In 1910, V. P. Semenov-Tyan-Shanski published another work entitled *Town and country in European Russia*. The originality and strength of the book lay in the fact that it linked together aspects of both uniform and nodal approaches to the concept of region. The focus was on settlement systems, which were characterized on the one hand by the background of the natural environment and the cultural landscape (the latter presented as uniform spatial units), and on the other hand, from the point of view of the role of urban places in their areas of influence. Types of villages and towns were classified according to functions they performed, and all this was discussed in the context of their historical development. The aim of the work was to divide European Russia into settlement regions; these were presented as combinations of uniform landscape regions, and the hinterlands of cities and towns as nodal spatial structures.

The regional paradigm did not develop on its own. It was paralleled by two other orientations (environmental determinism and possibilism), which dealt with the problem of man and his relation to the natural environment. These three approaches had much in common, as many problems that were posed while studying human existence within a geographical setting were verified using examples from regional studies, and generalizations from these studies, on the other hand, were adopted for the needs of environmental determinism and possibilism. This is the main reason that some aspects of the regional approach which have been presented here will be repeated in the next section where the paradigms concerning the relationship between human life and its physical setting are discussed.

Environmental determinism and possibilism

As with the paradigms described in the two sections above, environmental determinism and possibilism were approaches that emerged in the classical phase. Unlike the former, however, these approaches also underwent significant development during the modern stage, which is why this analysis distinguishes the two periods.

The classical period

It was a specific feature of geography in Russia that environmental determinism hardly developed in its most extreme form, as took place in Germany for example, and usually presented a well-balanced interpretation of the man–nature relationship (Hooson 1968).

As Anuchin (1960, 37) claims, environmental determinism in Russia appeared under the considerable influence of French materialism of the Enlightenment era. Known among Russian geographers were the theories of French thinkers concerning the dependence of social life on natural conditions: among others, Montesquieu's idea about the crucial role of climate in conditioning the character of political systems. At the same time, however, geographers in Russia were familiar with the ideas of Diderot, Helvetius and Holbach, who denied the decisive significance of geographical environment in influencing human affairs. The German school had an impact as well. There was known Kant's pioneering approach in which he broke with theological ways of thinking in geography. It is possible that his concept of physical geography concerning man's association with the natural environment, and human activity as an important factor in changes on the face of the earth, were not unfamiliar to Russian geographers. Anuchin (1960, 93) claims, however, that it was rather G. Rickert and his neo-Kantian ideas dealing with spatial relations as the main subject of geography, which had a greater influence on the discipline than Kant's point of view.

The first among scholars in Russia who pointed out the significance of the problem of the man–nature relationship for geographical studies was Lomonosov. According to him, the purpose of geography was to seek regularities among all the elements of the geographical environment, including man as its most important element (Anuchin 1960, 35). Lomonosov did not, however, define explicitly the character of the man–nature association. This may be, at the most, indirectly concluded from the way in which he interpreted the role of the human factor in geographical studies. These studies demonstrate that Lomonosov did not subordinate people to their physical setting. He analysed different patterns of human life and activity in space against the background of the natural environment; the latter was interpreted, however, as merely a complementary factor necessary to obtain a more complete picture of the geographical scene.

The first generalizations in Russian geography on the problem of how man and nature were interconnected appeared together with the regional studies. One of the first contributions to the problem was the book by Krashennikov about Kamchatka mentioned above. In it, he presented very thoroughly the severe conditions of the natural environment of the area and the way that people lived their lives there. The extreme character of the conditions provided many examples of the phenomenon of the subordination of man to the land, and this found its expression in his description of the region (Berg 1962).

At the same time generalizations started to emerge having a possibilistic character. Such was the approach proposed by Busching who initially divided the country into physical regions. He presented his point of view in his main work, *New earth description*, which went through eight editions from 1754 to 1792 (Buttner and Jakel 1982). In Busching's view, man was an element of a biological–physical whole which constituted the earth's surface. Man's connection with nature did not, however, take the form of dependence on physical conditions, 'but leaves him nevertheless greater or lesser opportunities for the training and improvement of his spiritual forces' (*ibid.*, 12). Between the cultural level of development of people, and the natural conditions, there was thus a specific interconnection which found its expression in both the traces which the physical setting left on human life, and the scale of transformation of the setting under the influence of human activity. For Busching, the main objective of geography was not so much to know about natural conditions, as to learn what humans had made of those conditions in any place in the world. The human aspect was central. In the conflict between natural preconditions and human actions, man's freedom of decision became predominant (Buttner and Jakel 1982).

In 1790, a book by N. Y. Cherepanov appeared entitled *Geographical and historical study*. Cherepanov proposed a two-way, reciprocal relationship between human activity and the impact of the environment. Man affected nature and transformed it through his agency, but the environment responded by influencing human life. In this mutual interdependence, both humans and their physical setting were subject to a process of permanent alteration. The process was not in complete balance both in time and space, however. At some times and in some places nature predominated, whereas in other times and areas humans were able to subordinate nature to their needs (Nikitin 1965b).

The above approach found its expression in the regional studies carried out in the first half of the nineteenth century where a similar significance was attributed to natural conditions and human characteristics. There was no predominance of either as criteria to distinguish a regional pattern. Such an approach was typical of the works of K. I. Arsenev and later P. P. Semenov-Tyan-Shanski.

In the second half of the century the major works of A. Humboldt and C. Ritter were translated and published in Russia (Nikitin 1966). The principle of causation as fundamental for geographical relations, the concept of geography as a chorological science, and a comparative method as a new way of scientific analysis propagated by these two scholars, became available and met with great interest among Russian geographers. The assumption about the causal character of links between humans and their physical environment proved to have a significant influence on the debate about the man–nature relationship. More works emerged concerning the problem. They primarily took the form of regional studies. The typical regional outline usually began with the location and position of a region and then proceeded through its geology, landforms, climate, vegetation, natural resources, settlement and cultural phenomena, and its economy and politics. Social, economic and political aspects were last in this chain as they were described and explained in terms of their physical base.

The above approach was opposed by the possibilists. They denied the passive role of humans in their geographical setting. People were able to behave actively, transforming the environment in which they lived. Such a point of view was proposed by N. G. Chernyshevski (1949). He emphasized the capability of people to change and transform natural conditions. Societies possessed, according to him, a specific 'energy of labour' which was the main factor in transforming nature. Different economic structures of society provided different energy of labour, and as a result there were distinct degrees to which the physical environment was transformed in various areas.

N. A. Dobrolubov claimed that the conditions of the geographical environment merely provided possibilities to be utilized; that very utilization, however, was related to the social conditions of human activity. These social conditions were not only the quality of life and cultural aspects of the way humans lived, but first of all the social positions of people and the relations among various social classes and groups conditioned by their economic situation. Dobrolubov opposed the concept of geography as a merely chorological science. He considered this approach to be one-sided, and pointed out the need to enrich the problem of spatial relations among places with the studies describing uniqueness of these places and the changes that moulded their character (Dobrolubov 1936).

The modern period

The establishment of the first department of geography at Moscow University in 1884 paved the way for the development of the discipline in a more professional way. The modern period within the paradigm being discussed here is distinguished from the modern as it was studied within the other two orientations in terms of a far larger variety and volume of work accomplished. This period was when the ideas of C. Darwin, D. Spencer and K. Marx had a profound influence on forming a new approach in social sciences, and in geography F. Ratzel and Vidal de la Blache introduced a new subdiscipline, anthropogeography, which later was known as human geography. All these changes were followed by geographers in Russia, but the discipline they developed was based primarily on their own achievements. This was seen particularly well in the field of speculation on the problem of the relationship between external physical conditions and the social life of man.

The above problem was concerned largely with a new field of geographical inquiry which, by analogy with the term applied in West European geography, was called anthropogeography. The name was introduced by D. N. Anuchin, who was appointed to the first chair of geography in 1884 and headed the Department of Geography and Ethnography at Moscow University. Anthropologist, ethnographer and archaeologist, he had a great interest in geography too, establishing what Esakov (1978) calls the Russian school of geography at the University of Moscow. He was also the founder of the journal *Physical Geography*, which soon became the main arena where Russian anthropogeographers published their work (Esakov 1978).

Anuchin was not so much a research worker, as a teacher involved in education and the popularization of geographical knowledge. In his outlook on geography he relied firmly on the ideas of Humboldt, Ritter, Richthofen and Reclus, being influenced also by Darwinism. As Esakov (1978) notices, the latter was the main methodological foundation of all Anuchin's work. Anuchin divided the subject matter of geography into three major parts: inorganic nature (physical geography without biography), organic nature (biogeography), and anthropogeography (human activity and culture in their physical surroundings). He did not consider these parts separately, however. For him, geography was the study of organic unity, the synthesis of physical, biotic and cultural phenomena on the earth's surface. This implied that anthropogeography as a division within the discipline was not an isolated field of inquiry as proposed by F. Ratzel, but an inseparable part of geography concerning the human aspects of geographical phenomena. The task of the discipline was to study the changing character of phenomena on the face of the earth. Phenomena and processes moulding the earth's surface should be analysed from the viewpoint of their origins and relations with one another. 'An adequate understanding of a country's surface forms, its landscape and life can only be attained by examining its past and studying those processes that have led to subsequent changes' (*ibid.*, 3). Man was, for Anuchin, the fundamental component of the nature, and 'the human element can never be excluded from geographical study, for human activity is reflected in many distinct features of the landscape' (*ibid.*, 3).

Anuchin's interest in the cultural landscape developed with time as he focused increasingly on regional geography which he distinguished from general geography. Region with its distinct landscape was the object whose studying enabled the geographer to analyse local aspects of general phenomena on the surface of the earth. In the case of a particular region, the environment in a specific way influenced human life and activity, but these in their turn imprinted characteristic traces on the physiognomy of the natural surroundings, creating a human landscape. Regional study should examine this reciprocal interconnection, to provide 'the fullest and most complete portrait of a region, its natural conditions, population, culture, position and significance among other regions' (Anuchin in Hooson 1968, 264).

The first large work concerning the man–nature problem that appeared in the paradigm in the modern period was the book of I. Mechnikov, *Civilization and great historical streams*. It greatly influenced a number of his contemporaries, particularly E. Reclus (the book was written in Switzerland) and people from Reclus' circle. The work was published posthumously by Reclus in 1889 (in Russian in 1898), and many of its ideas found their expression in his *Geographie universelle*. A hot advocate of Mechnikov's approach was Plekhanov, who drew inspiration from the book to formulate his theses concerning the environmental foundations of historical materialism (Nikitin 1965c).

In his book, Mechnikov considered large rivers and sea shores as crucial factors of the geographical environment conditioning the course of history of human societies. According to the role which waterways played in the progress of human civilization, he distinguished three periods within the history of mankind: river, Mediterranean and ocean civilization. In the beginning, history developed along the larger rivers which were the arteries of life and civilization in ancient Egypt, Mesopotamia, India and China. Later, civilization centred on the Mediterranean basin, then distributed itself in the third period along ocean shores. Much of the book concerns the role of large rivers in the history of civilization, which Mechnikov interpreted as a synthesis of natural conditions (Nikitin 1965c).

According to him, the aim of the book was to demonstrate 'the relations and mutual interdependence between the particular physico-geographical environment and different stages of social evolution or periods of collective history of humanity'. Further on he declared, we are by no means advocates of the theory of geographical fatalism which proclaims in defiance of facts that a particular aggregate of physico-geographical conditions plays and has to play the same unchanged role. No, the problem is to define the historical importance of these conditions as well as the variability of this importance in the course of centuries and at different stages of civilization. (Nikitin 1965c, 366.)

In the opinion of Anuchin (1960, 43),

Mechnikov undoubtedly committed some geographical-determinism errors, nevertheless he was able to understand the reciprocal character of the relations between society and nature [. . .] Bringing forward a geographical factor as a 'driving force of history' Mechnikov always asserted that the influence of this factor manifested itself not immediately but in the mutual relationship between society and nature, in the process of social production.

A significant contribution to the debate concerning the question of the interdependence between nature and human society was made by A. I. Voyeykov. He was a famous climatologist, the creator of many modern branches of climatology including agro-climatology. His interest in human aspects of the natural environment developed from studying the climatic conditions of various regions of Russia and the impact of these conditions on human activity. He was particularly interested in the geography of population, the distribution of people on the face of the earth and the factors underlying this distribution. Much of his analysis included social and economic factors. He tried to find the reasons governing the pattern by which people allocate territory by studying peculiarities of migration and urbanization, the localization of food production, the degree of intensity of transformation of the environment by human activity, and the influence of social relations. For him it was obvious that only part of these reasons was related to the physical environment, and without taking economic and social factors into account it was impossible to understand human phenomena in space. Voyeykov's ultimate conclusion was : 'the decisive factor in the distribution of population is not so much the natural surroundings as man himself' (Pokshishevski 1965).

While analysing the relationship between society and nature, Voyeykov emphasized the need to study dynamic aspects and to find the genetic roots of every phenomenon. This approach he applied in his famous book of 1909 entitled *The population of settlements of European Russia and Western Siberia* where, besides detailed quantitative (statistical) analysis of demographic phenomena, he presented an extensive description of the qualitative features of settlement, together with all factors of an economic, social, cultural and historical character conditioning settlement patterns. According to Pokshishevski (1965) it was an almost unique work in Russian literature. It presented with great skill the relationship of settlement to various cultural landscapes of Russia which were expressively and accurately analysed from the point of view of the process of their historical formation.

After the October Revolution and the emergence of the Soviet state, the problem of the man–nature association was practically banned from geographical debate as contradictory to the vein of the new Marxist-based paradigm which seized the discipline at that time and which denied any connection between social phenomena and the physical environment. Nevertheless, the former paradigms were not ousted at once, and a few valuable works appeared whose nature was still in accord with the developments of the modern period concerning the problem of the man–nature relationship.

The first among these works was the book by A. A. Kruber entitled *General geography* (Kruber 1923). The book consisted of three volumes. Two-and-a-half of them concerned diverse aspects of physical geography, and the other half of the third volume only was devoted to anthropogeography. For Kruber, the latter category dealt with the study of people against the background of the physical environment they occupied. In different places people lived different ways of life because natural conditions compelled them to adapt in a distinctive way to what Kruber called the laws of nature. People should obey these laws in order to survive, and in this sense they were determined by the external physical environment like plants and animals. People were able, however, to comprehend these laws and, unlike the rest of the living world, make use of nature's gifts; this helped them to adapt to the physical environment and to choose their ways of life (Kruber 1923).

In 1924 *Essays in economic geography* by S. V. Bernstein-Kogan was published. According to Bernstein-Kogan, the task of economic geography was to identify types of regions, study individual regions and analyse regional interaction. The concept of region was based on that of landscape and was interpreted as the territorial combination of economic and cultural phenomena as well as natural conditions. By analogy with landscape types, Bernstein-Kogan identified and classified different types of regions. This classification started by delimiting natural spatial units, uniform in terms of climatic and biotic features, and then, by adding economic and cultural criteria, regional landscapes were distinguished within the framework of the physical division. Studying individual regions consisted in tracing the history of their development in order to identify factors lying behind the contemporary composition of phenomena constituting regional landscapes. Different types of regions, each region with its own history, created spatial systems interconnected by relations of various kinds which should be studied to understand both particular regions and their systems as a whole (Bernstein-Kogan 1924).

Perhaps the largest among the works that still related to the modern period and which appeared in the Soviet geography was *Region and country*, published by V. P. Semenov-Tyan-Shanski in 1928. The book was the most complete and comprehensive presentation of theoretical developments in Russian geography. According to Semenov-Tyan-Shanski, geography was 'a fully independent science studying the laws of spatial relations of life on earth in the broad sense of the word, i.e. from the life of rocks to the life of man' (Kaganski *et al.* 1980, 359). Such a broad approach implied, however, that much of the subject matter of the discipline pertained to other non-geographical sciences. The geographers' task was therefore to generalize, in terms of spatial pattern, all the information they gathered. Spatial pattern was governed at the same time by the laws of spatial location. These constituted the theoretical system of the discipline. Geographers should seek these laws, and one of the efficient ways of doing this was a well-elaborated methodology of classification. As Kaganski *et al.* (1980) assert, Semenov-Tyan-Shanski formulated about sixty geographical laws, of which twenty were discussed in his book.

According to Semenov-Tyan-Shanski, there were two major concepts crucial to geographical analysis: man and space. The first was the subject of geography, 'the measure of all things, giving meaning to geographical synthesis' (*ibid.*, 359). This synthesis, in turn, consisted in joining into one, functional system all physical conditions (organic and inorganic), all the forms of economy and all events of ethnopolitical geography. Such a system was composed of a variety of relations, of particular importance being those among people and those among people and things in their geographical environment. Both kinds of relations were of interest to anthropogeography where man was treated, not only as the element of the natural setting, but also as an active agent transforming his physical surroundings. Among relations of the geographical system, Semenov-Tyan-Shanski distinguished also those which allowed geographers to define this system as chorological in its nature. There were also relations of static and dynamic character, the latter taking the form of flows, movements and transformations which were integral parts of any geographical phenomenon and the main reason for its change. A specific was the concept of so-called dynamic statistics which were relatively immobile structures formed by sets of flows; Semenov-Tyan-Shanski considered regions as presenting structures of this kind (Kaganski *et al.* 1980).

Despite the formal character of many considerations, the book provided at the same time a valuable insight into problems of humanistic geography. As an anthropogeographer, Semenov-Tyan-Shanski attached great significance to man's integration with his environment. For him, the phenomena in which people and nature were combined in the clearest form were landscapes. Landscape was an 'all-important, all-essential and all-encompassing aspect of geography as a science, bringing it close to the fine arts and endowing it with that indispensable artistic element that distinguishes geography from many other sciences' (Semenov-Tyan-Shanski in Kaganski *et al.* 1980, 362). The geographer, like the artist, should think in terms of geographic images and be able to express the emotional and inspiring impact of various types of landscape. Semenov-Tyan-Shanski wrote about geographical *paysages*, the geography of sounds and smells, about the aesthetic resources of nature. All this should be taken into account to understand, describe and explain how humans were interconnected with places they occupied (Kaganski *et al.* 1980, 362).

The last work referring to anthropogeographical traditions which was published in the Soviet period was the book by L. S. Berg entitled *Landscape-geographical zones of the USSR*, published in 1930. In its essence, the book echoed the major theses of the author's view of geography which he presented in 1913 in his lecture to the Geographical Society. He defined then the landscape as the main subject matter of the discipline, distinguishing between natural and cultural landscapes and assuming that the essence of the latter was various forms of human settlement. The concept of landscape was a fundamental category organizing the reasoning/argument presented in his book. For Berg, 'geographical landscape is such assemblage or aggregate of things and phenomena in which peculiarities of the relief, climate, waters, flora and fauna and also human activity merge into one harmonic whole, typically repeating over a particular area' (Berg in Pokshishevski 1965, 505).

In the book, detailed characteristics of particular landscape-geographical zones in the USSR were presented, each zone analysed in terms of physical and human geography. The latter geography concerned population, its activity, and diverse aspects of human culture outlined on the basis of rich ethnographic material (Pokshishevski 1965). Ethnographic and economic differences among zones were discussed against the background of natural conditions. Berg, however, did not explain these differences in terms of the influence of the landscape only. He was aware of the significance of social and economic factors in shaping the pattern of cultural and social content of particular areas. Berg's proposition of the typology of geographical disciplines which dealt with the description of landscapes was interesting. Among these disciplines he distinguished anthropogeography or the geography of man and his culture. Anthropogeography, in turn, was subdivided into the geography of races and nations (anthropological geography) and the geography of culture (ethnographical geography).

Within the latter he identified economic geography, which described geographical landscape from the point of view of its economic life in relation to both the natural environment and other economic regions (Pokshishevski 1965, 507).

Modern geography in Eastern Europe

Modern geography in Eastern Europe started to develop in the last three decades of the nineteenth century. Although the first chair of geography had been established earlier in 1849 at Krakow University in Poland, it was abolished after four years and restored only in 1871 (Babicz 1978). By the end of the 1870s there were two departments of geography in the country; the other was at Lwow University. In 1873 geography was introduced in the University of Budapest (Enyedi 1964), and in 1883 and 1893 two chairs of geography were founded in Zagreb and Belgrade respectively (Roglic 1952). A department of geography was created at the university in Prague in 1891. By the end of the decade geography was established at the university in Sofia in 1898 and the University of Bucharest in 1900. There were thus at the turn of the century two departments of geography in what later became Poland, and two in what was to become Yugoslavia, as well as one department in Bulgaria, one in Romania, and one each in the territories of the future Hungary and Czechoslovakia. By the end of the 1920s, when all the countries in the region were independent, the number of universities in which geography was taught had grown considerably. In Poland four new departments had been founded: in Warszawa and Poznan in 1919, Lublin in 1920 and Wilno in 1925. In Yugoslavia, besides the departments of geography in Zagreb and Belgrade, new ones were opened in Skopje in 1921 and Ljubljana in 1920. Also in Romania, the number of universities with geographical departments increased to four. They were founded in Iasi in 1904, Cluj in 1919 and Cernautsi in 1920. Two new departments of geography were established in Hungary, one at the Faculty of Political Economy in Budapest in 1919 and the other at the University of Debrecen in 1914. Only in Bulgaria and Czechoslovakia had no further departments emerged. The only country where geography came into being after the First World War was Estonia. Here the only geographical department in the Baltic states was founded in Tartu in 1919.

The introduction of geography was a new field of learning in the universities was accompanied by the emergence of geographical societies whose basic aim was to propagate and disseminate geographical knowledge as well as to organize and develop geographical education of all kinds. The societies issued their own journals which complemented the more

professionally-oriented publications of the universities. The first geographical society was founded in Romania and Hungary in 1875, followed by
those in Czechoslovakia in 1895, Poland in 1906 and Serbia in 1910.

At around the same time the first ideas and concepts of modern geography
were appearing in Western Europe, primarily in Germany and France.
These were firmly rooted in the conceptual system created by A. Humboldt
and C. Ritter, and then developed by their successors: F. Richthofen, F.
Ratzel and A. Hettner in Germany and P. Vidal de la Blache and his co-
workers in France. They, like Humboldt and Ritter, saw geography as the
discipline concerning the mutual connection of diverse phenomena on the
earth's surface. For German geographers in particular, physical features of
land were the context in which man's activity was embedded, and geography
was a unified category studying how human life was organized under the
influence of the physical environment. Richthofen and Ratzel, the latter
in the first phase of his career, have often been credited with developing
environmental determinism when stressing the decisive role of physical
features in the evolution of human societies. Later, Ratzel changed his
point of view (mainly under the influence of A. Kirchhoff, who saw the
primary focus of geography in the relation of man to the physical earth,
but emphasized the importance of human activity rather than the impact
of the natural environment). Ratzel adopted this approach in his second
volume of *Anthropogeographie* published in 1891. Ideas of his new
anthropogeography became the first step in dividing geography into physical
geography and what was soon called 'human geography' (James and Martin
1981, 168–9). The latter term was introduced by Vidal de la Blache.
Vidal's concern was the problem of why people adapted better to one
place than to others. For him, it was not so much the influence of the natural
environment (*milieu*), as the way in which humans were able to make use
of the diversity of possibilities that nature offered them. They selected
those possibilities which best fitted their cultural dispositions, or more
generally, their way of life (*genre de vie*). When confronted with particular
physical conditions, various ways of life produced specific cultural landscapes (*pays*). Their emergence in the process of mutual interplay between
ways of human life and *milieux* in which this life was conducted was the
major goal of human geography studies (Buttimer 1971, 52–7).

There were many students from Eastern Europe at that time studying
under leading German and French geographers. Most of these students
later became professors in their countries. They were strongly engaged
personally in not only creating the necessary institutional conditions to
teach geography (often being offered chairs of geography in newly-
opened universities), but also in propagating intensively the knowledge
they acquired during their studies. It was largely under their influence,

and later that of their students, that new ideas in geography swept rapidly over Eastern Europe and dominated the way in which geography was pursued in the subregion.

Four paradigms developed within East European geography in the modern period. These were, on the one hand, the orientations related to the problem of the man–nature relationship, namely environmental determinism, possibilism and indeterminism, and on the other hand, the regional paradigm. Another paradigm – exploration – was widely applied in some western countries and Russia, but was virtually ignored by geographers in the subregion. Some of them participated in exploration, especially in the nineteenth century, when expeditions were frequently organized by German, Russian and Austrian geographical societies. Later, when independent, some countries sent expeditions to other parts of the world, but this activity was relatively insignificant. The main research paradigms are presented in the remainder of this chapter.

Environmental determinism, possibilism and indeterminism

Within the debate on the problem of the relationship between man and his environment, three paradigms developed in East European geography in the modern period. They appeared chronologically in the following sequence: environmental determinism, possibilism and environmental indeterminism.

Environmental determinism

This was the first paradigm applied by geographers in the subregion, providing an explanation of the patterns of human life and activity on the surface of the earth. Assumptions of this paradigm were, almost without exception, borrowed from German geography, from the works of both its classical period (Humboldt and Ritter) as well as its modern period (Richthofen, Ratzel and Hettner). Geographers in the subregion applied not merely the assumptions; they also employed the methodology of geographical inquiry initially developed within the German school. This was more or less a standard scheme according to which geographical description and explanation were provided. The description started with detailed analysis of the natural environment. Thus, geology, landforms and surface features, climate, vegetation and waters were described first, creating a physical context in terms of which social and economic phenomena were examined. These were settlement, population, forms of economic life and political organization of the territorial society. Explanation was based on the assumption that there was a causal connection between the physical base and the social world, and studies were undertaken to identify regularities confirming this hypothesis.

There were undoubtedly important circumstances conducive to a generally favourable reception of the paradigm among East European geographers. On the one hand, there was the character of the natural environment of a large part of the subregion. Local and regional variations of the man-made world and their convergence with physical forms were frequently very salient and stimulating, especially in areas with pronounced topographical variety. On the other hand, in conditions of the virtual lack of economic growth in this part of Europe, patterns of human occupation of space remained almost unchanged for long periods, prompting a search for reasons lying in the sphere of natural phenomena rather than in the social and economic environment.

The paradigm was not pursued in isolation. There were firm connections with the regional approach, and this found its expression in using such basic categories of the regional orientation as region, landscape and settlement to verify environmental generalizations.

The earliest traces of employing this paradigm can be found in the work of the Polish geographer W. Pol, the first scholar in Eastern Europe to teach geography (at Krakow University beginning in 1849). This was only the second academic appointment in geography in the world, following Ritter's chair in Berlin in 1820. In his approach, Pol was influenced primarily by the ideas of Humboldt and Ritter. Geography was seen as a unified field dealing with people and their activities in the natural environment. The task of the geographer was to provide a detailed and integrated account of all the components of the physical land as the natural conditions around which human life was organized (Babicz 1978).

Later, studies within the paradigm in Poland concerned two major problems. On the one side, these were investigations dealing with causal connections between various forms of human occupation in space and the characteristics of the natural environment; on the other side was the particular problem of accounting for the rights of the Polish nation to the land it inhabited. The former studies tended to explain how diverse patterns of settlement (as the most distinguishable form in which human existence in space manifested itself) were conditioned by features of the natural setting. The analysis of geographical location and conditions determining the phenomenon was undertaken largely in terms of historical evolution and concerned both rural and urban forms of settlement (Dziewonski 1956; Kielczewska-Zalewska 1964).

The problem of the right of the nation to its land acquired considerable importance in the difficult contemporary political situation. Geographers contributed substantially to the elucidation of many controversial issues, making use of existing geographical schemes of explanation based on the concept of environmental determinism. Well known was the activity of the leading Polish geographer E. Romer, who presented and defended (using geographical and historical arguments) the justification of the Polish state at the Paris peace conference, and later wrote much on how the cultural, economic and social characteristics of the Polish nation and its history were related to distinct natural features of the territory between the Baltic Sea and the Black Sea (Babicz 1977). The arguments of other Polish geographers were similar, among which a work by S. Lencewicz entitled *The anthropogeographical border of Poland* was distinguished by 'its originality and comprehensiveness' (Kondracki 1981).

Very similar was the character of environmental studies in Romania. As in Poland, there was on the one hand an interest in the problem of the relationship of man to the physical land, and on the other, attempts to demonstrate in terms of the generalizations provided by the paradigm the validity of links between the Romanian peeople and their historical territory. Studies of the man–nature relationship were originated by S. Mehedinti, the founder of the Romanian school of geography and the first academic teacher of the discipline in the country. The accent was on determinism, particularly in the earlier period of his activity. He presented and interpreted the relationships among major components of the geographical environment as causal in character, and emphasized the significance of the natural setting (particularly relief) in conditioning the distribution of other elements and in determining human life and activity (Mihailescu 1977). This interest in environmental determinism was soon replaced by the possibilist perspective, and major works of Mehedinti were concerned primarily with the latter orientation.

Leading Romanian geographers who later pursued the discipline together with Mehedinti were largely his students. They followed the ideas he proposed and applied, and thus their involvement in environmental determinism was not great. Some tended to use this paradigm, however. The most valuable studies within the paradigm concerned the interconnection between human life and culture and the conditions of the natural environment. One of the first was a work by A. D. Aldem entitled *Man and environment in the Carpathians* (Cotet 1979), followed later by investigations by other geographers into temporary settlement and pasture culture in mountainous areas of the country (Popp 1938).

Deterministic approaches found wide applicability in studies of the ties that connected a nation with the land it occupied. Perhaps the most significant contribution to the problem was the investigations carried out by I. Conea. He examined various aspects of human activity with respect to the physical environment in the province of Transylvania, finding evidence confirming its attachment to the Romanian nation. Conea studied the relationships between settlement and topography, as well as migration and conditions of the natural environment, to show how physical factors influenced patterns of human occupation within the area and were conducive in maintaining the old national culture in this part of the country (Turnock 1984).

Elsewhere in Eastern Europe, geography developed from the ideas and concepts of one scholar. In Yugoslavia the geographer who originated the discipline was J. Cvijic, the founder of the department of geography at the university in Belgrade. His studies, like those of Mehedinti, were originally focused on the problem of the causal relationships between the natural world and human life and activity. There were two fields where his deterministic point of view found partial expression. First, he analysed cultural regions, which he interpreted in terms of the adaptation of cultural groups to specific geographical conditions, showing how the distribution of the groups was conditioned by areas having natural barriers (Cvijic 1918). Secondly, he investigated rural settlements, seeking to demonstrate how the location of rural habitats was related to the natural features of the land (Vasovic 1980).

This approach was continued later by other Yugoslavian geographers, such as A. Melik and S. Ilesic. Melik specialized in geomorphology and then trained in ethnography and history, allowing him to undertake a comprehensive analysis of the problem of how man and nature were combined into one organic unity using examples primarily from areas of rural settlement (Thomas 1985). Ilesic was also involved in studies of settlement patterns and primarily investigated their evolution. He sought to find connections between the Slovenian nation and its land, and worked within the deterministic paradigm to provide the evidence for his hypotheses (Thomas 1987).

In other countries of the subregion, studies within the paradigm developed in a very similar way although with less intensity. In Bulgaria, a similar approach was applied by A. Ishirkov, the founder of geography at the university in Sofia, and Ratzel's disciple. He examined the relation of various cultural aspects of human life to the geographical environment in his studies of the human landscape. Ishirkov, and later his students, investigated diverse landscapes in Bulgaria and sought to demonstrate, by applying historical analysis, how different complexes of physical factors made emerging areal units distinct, from the point of view of the combination of their natural and man-made content (Ocovsky 1969).

In Czechoslovakia, studies of a deterministic nature were initiated by J. Palacky who introduced geography into the university in Prague and was the first teacher of the discipline. Having a firm historical background, he focused on the problem of the role of the natural environment in the history of the country and tried to find geographical evidence of its impact within settlement phenomena.

The greatest contribution to the paradigm in Hungary was the book by Czirbusz on *Human geography*. It consisted of three volumes and was published in 1915–19. In the first two volumes named *Influence of landforms* and *Anthropogeography*, he presented the contemporary state of the art in the discipline and the influence of the German school. Using settlement as the most pronounced element of human landscape, the ideas and approaches were applied concerning the problem of man's relation to his physical environment.

Possibilism

As in Western Europe, possibilism emerged in East European geography as a reaction to the generalizations of environmental determinism. This new paradigm appeared mainly under the influence of Vidal de la Blache and the French school of geography he created. Possibilism started to develop in the first decade of the twentieth century and soon complemented the deterministic approach. However, studies carried out within the new orientation did not differ much from those of the older paradigm. They were outlines of the areal differentiation of human life and activity against the background of the features of the physical environment. The character of the approach was distinct, however. There was no causal relationship assumed, such that human life was subordinated to the landscape. Fundamental was the idea that there was a balance between physical and natural factors. People were controlled by the environment, but at the same time they modified their physical setting according to their cultural dispositions and material capabilities (Nowakowski 1934).

In Poland, studies of the geographical environment in terms of the limits it set and the possibilities it offered for human life and activity began relatively early. It may well be that these earlier attempts to seek an explanation outside a deterministic approach were the consequence of the less pronounced topographical differentiation of the Polish landscape, providing less evidence (as compared with other countries in the subregion) to support a deterministic point of view. The first investigations were initiated by Potkanski (1922), who stressed the significance of other factors aside from natural environment, such as the degree of economic development, as well as the quantity (mainly density) and quality of population that influenced the character of human occupation in space. Potkanski applied his point of view in his study of the evolution of settlement patterns, demonstrating how the spatial distribution of human habitats reflected the process of adaptation to the conditions produced by nature. Investigations by Mrazkowna (1922), Kielczewska (1937), Leszczycki (1937) and Pawlowski and Czekalski (1937) widened this point of view concerning a larger variety of forms of human settlement as well as the natural, social, historical and economic characteristics of both the population and the surrounding environment.

Whereas in Poland, studies within this paradigm were carried out from the beginning by a number of scholars, in Romania they were initiated by Mehedinti and later followed by his disciples. Mehedinti was a student of Vidal de la Blache, and this undoubtedly had a significant influence on his scientific orientation. He presented his point of view in his main work, *Terra: theoretical and general geography* published in 1930. Mehedinti saw geography as a unitary field whose subject matter was the external shell of the earth composed of four terrestial spheres: litosphere, atmosphere, hydrosphere and biosphere (the last including man). They were interconnected by a network of mutual relations constituting a functional and dynamic whole. Such a wholeness was characteristic not only of the entire earth's surface, but of every area within it. Each region or area was an intersection through all the four spheres and presented a functional and dynamic composition that was the environment in which human life and activity were conducted. Man was fully integrated with his environment, and this integration had a balanced character. This meant that the dynamics of the natural setting had the form not only of changes within human phenomena caused by physical factors, but also of changes on the face of the earth resulting from human action. This point of view Mehedinti emphasized when he formulated the purpose of geography. According to him, it was 'to recognize and understand areal units, including their inhabitants and the effect of human activity on their surface, for the form, structure and dynamism of such units provide the environment in which human life develops, inevitably interacting with the complexity of their conditions' (Mihailescu 1977, 67).

Mehedinti was concerned with the problem of human ability and activity in shaping the natural world in another of his works entitled *Le pays et le peuple Roumain*, published in 1927. Using the example of Romania, he stated that every area had its specific individuality or personality which was the consequence of the combination of the natural conditions and resources. How to use and utilize these resources depended on the quality of people living there. This quality was a combination of a variety of features, among which he distinguished the continuum of the nation, its homogeneity, its attitude to life, its political organization and its organic unity. After characterizing Romanian people and the natural conditions of their country, Mehedinti presented its economic and political situation as the result of the interplay of both natural and human factors (Mihailescu 1977).

The ideas of Mehedinti were continued by his disciples. Perhaps the best known were C. Bratescu and G. Valsan. Both were trained in geomorphology and were able, at the same time, to work in every field of the discipline including human geography. For Bratescu, the objective of the discipline was to study both the physical environment as the geographical setting of man, and the phenomenon of human agency which resulted in the transformation of natural land (Nimigeanu 1980). Valsan had a similar view of geography. 'Between people and their environment there is an uninterrupted interaction so that the evolution of people is not passively imposed by the environment but is rather an active and continuous adaptation, a compromise between environmental guidelines and the response given by any ethnic organism' (Popp 1978, 129). According to Valsan, the phenomenon of the impact of nature on human life was far less difficult to study than the responses of people to this influence. 'It is much easier to assess the relationship between the environment and the density of population than to discern in the ethos of people what makes them respond to physical factors such as relief, climate and waters' (Popp 1978, 129). Valsan held that the latter problem could be well approached only with the assistance of other social sciences, and he was a keen advocate of studies that connected geographical, sociological and ethnographical perspectives (Popp 1978).

Possibilistic approaches in Yugoslavian geography were originated by J. Cvijic. The basic assumptions of the approach were presented in his major book *La peninsule Balcanique* published in 1918 (Vasovic 1980). The work examined the geographical environment and its influence on the lives of people, as well as the changing impact of human society on the natural surroundings. Cvijic created a model of human geography which had much in common with *la tradition Vidalienne*, although Vasovic (1980) holds that Cvijic's work was entirely original. Cvijic distinguished six main research areas in his human geography: zones of culture and civilization, distribution and migration of population, types of economic life, situation and types of buildings, classification of house types, and ethnic and psychological attributes of South Slavs (Vasovic 1980, 27).

Zones of culture and civilization were marked by the traces that past civilizations or cultural groups had imprinted on their physical setting. The latter was an important factor. When firmly differentiated, it enhanced the distinctiveness of cultural zones; otherwise this distinction was difficult to identify. What was not conducive to the maintenance of these zones, and erased earlier established cultural landscapes, were the movements of people. Cvijic tried to explain, using the concept of cultural zones and migration, the apparently complex mosaic of peoples living in Yugoslavia, and he employed an historical approach to reconstruct the way in which the two phenomena were connected with each other.

Much work was done by Cvijic on the classification of rural settlement, not only in Yugoslavia, but also all over the Balkan peninsula. His original classification of towns is based on the typology of cultural zones he prepared earlier. In categorizing rural settlement he took into account not only cultural aspects (situation and types of buildings and classification of house types), but also natural factors whose impact was very significant in the differentiated topography of the Balkan countries.

Cvijic focused considerable attention on ethnic problems. He defined ethnic groups in terms of the 'psychic' character of the population and its culture, which he studied from many points of view. He was interested in the views of life, religious allegiance, folklore, dialects, costumes and other features of human habits and customs (Freeman 1966, Vasovic 1980).

Much empirical work was provided by Cvijic in various parts of Serbia according to the conceptual model he elaborated. Data on settlement and buildings, local economy, life and culture were assembled. 'From all this came twenty-five monographs on the origin and life of the people and as a result Serbia became one of the best studied countries of the world' (Vasovic 1980, 29). This model of studies was then continued by Yugoslavian geographers in the modern period. The regional studies in particular took over much from Cvijic's ideas of human geography and were distinguished by their orginality within the subregion.

In Hungary, investigations of the mutual interplay between humans and their natural environment were initiated by P. Teleki. He was particularly interested in the ethnographic characteristics of the population and the tracks which human culture had imprinted on the natural environment. Teleki used the outcomes of his studies to delimit areas 'marked by the cultural development and tradition of Hungarian people', and his work resulted in the publication of a number of maps of the cultural and human regions of the country (Kish 1987). Another Hungarian geographer, J. Cholnoky, applied possibilistic assumptions in his studies of the regional geography of the Great Hungarian Lowland. The peculiarities in ways of life caused by both the impact of physical conditions and the influence of people on their geographical surroundings were analysed in order to delimit the region and define its natural and cultural parts (Cholnoky 1910).

In Czechoslovakia the first possibilistic studies were initiated by Dvorsky (1923). He pointed to the significance of various aspects of the cultural and economic history of the population in different local areas in producing the diversity of settlement pattern which led, in turn, to emerging differences in cultural landscapes. Kral (1932) studied man as an agent transforming the geographical setting and the development of man's growing impact on the natural environment from the conditions of a primitive human landscape to a highly-developed cultural landscape.

In Bulgaria, investigations of the geographical environment in terms of the limits it set and possibilities it offered for human life and activity were initiated by the disciples of A. Ishirkov. Zachariev (1928) was the first to use the assumptions of the paradigm in his studies of the process of formation of human landscapes in the country. Similar were the investigations of Batakliev (1938) and Gonchev (1938), who analysed settlement patterns in various parts of Bulgaria and explained the differences from the point of view of not only the influence of natural factors, but also certain characteristics of people, such as their customs, habits, attitude to work and land, as well as some ethnographic traits.

Environmental indeterminism

According to Anuchin (1960, 55), environmental or geographical indeterminism consists in the detachment of the objective world from its material base and treating it as a subjective entity, a construct created by the human mind. The geographical environment from this point of view is a mental image, a product of human consciousness experienced by the subject who is either an individual or a social group.

The indeterminist paradigm developed in the East European subregion in the form of two approaches. The first approach, the so-called theory of the perceptual environment, was introduced and applied in Estonia by J. G. Grano. The second approach had a humanistic character, and was formulated and developed in Poland by F. Znaniecki.

Grano was a Finnish geographer who in 1919 was offered the chair of geography at a newly reopened University of Tartu. He stayed there until 1923 when he returned to Helsinki as a professor of geography. During that time, he developed his view of geography as a unitary discipline with well-defined subject matter which were geographical areas representing man's perceptual environment. His ideas he described in the book entitled *Reine geographie* which was published in 1929 (Grano 1979).

According to Grano, the essential object of geographical studies were areal units (landscapes) presenting integrity of human and natural components. These were not objective entities, however, but the structures or complexes perceived by a subject. Only in this way could their holistic character be grasped because the descriptions produced by specialists from systematic disciplines failed to reflect the integrity or interrelation of phenomena constituting a landscape. Grano derived this point of view from psychology. Generalizations made in this science convinced him that it was possible to consider landscape as a holistic entity presenting an impression of the environment.

In terms of his theory of the perceptual environment, Grano was able to interpret the problem of the man–nature relationship, not as a causal or possibilistic interaction, but as 'the reciprocity of man's mind and his surroundings' (Grano 1979, 76). Man's environment was the sum totality of sensations provided by the real world. According to Grano, the sensations perceived by all man's senses produced the immediate surroundings; landscape was a distant environment observed only through sight. Outside the landscape and the perceptual environment there existed the real world, and Grano's main problem was to embed his concept of man's subjective environment in the objectively existing world. To this end he introduced the idea of the region. The objective environment 'that encircles man everywhere and continually, both his immediate surroundings and the landscape, and which moves with the individual observer, has to be fixed in space to the surface of the earth, to areal units as homogeneous complexes. These Grano called not landscapes, but geographical regions (Grano 1979, 76). The task of geography was to delimit regions and to describe them. This was not a matter of discovering regions, since these were determined arbitrarily; rather, it was a question of defining them. This Grano presented in his work using rich empirical material he collected in Estonia. Employing various cartographical techniques, he was able to present regional structures in terms of the concept of core areas and transition zones. He was also able to express in a cartographic way sensory impressions attached to various places in space, thereby describing and mapping landscape regions in Estonia (Grano 1979).

As James and Martin (1981, 251) observe, 'Grano followed Schluter in identifying the landscape as that part of the natural surroundings of man that can be perceived by the senses'. But no geographer at that time formulated a comprehensive theoretical approach to the problem of environmental perception. It was only Grano who, in 1922, introduced what much later came to be known as behavioural geography.

Grano based his theory on the assumption that there were two worlds existing separately: an objective world outside the observer, not susceptible to distortion by subjective acts of perception, and a subjective world imagined in the human mind. The humanistic approach that emerged later in Poland assumed that there was only one world combining both those mentioned above. The environment was not opposed to man, that is, it did not exist as an entity beyond man's consciousness. Interpreted as the outside world, the environment acted only in relation to man's image. Such an approach to the problem of man's relation to his environment was first proposed by the outstanding Polish sociologist F. Znaniecki in his little-known paper entitled 'Sociological foundations of human ecology', published in 1938. In fact he had presented elements of his approach in 1931 when he introduced his humanistic theory of the urban environment. This theory emerged both as a reaction and an alternative to Park's urban ecology. Unlike Park and his followers, who considered the urban area as an objective socio-spatial structure, Znaniecki interpreted the territory of the city as a humanistic whole being formed in human experience and activity. People indeed occupy urban space, 'but they are not only objects but active subjects being able to experience what is around them, and from this point of view they are not within the city but, if one may say so, the city is in their common sphere of experience and activity, they create it as a complex structure' (Znaniecki 1931, ix–x).

Znaniecki presented his humanistic theory of space in a fuller version in his later work already mentioned above (Znaniecki 1938). Here he made a distinction between geographical and humanistic space. They were the only ones existing in the practice of the social sciences. The first was absolute, featureless, objectively measurable, limitless and infinitely divisible. People and patterns of material things were distributed within it, and processes occurred to change existing spatial structures. From the humanistic point of view, on the other hand, there was no such thing as an absolute space. 'Space for a humanist is one of many categories which he uses studying man. It is analogous to a myth, language, ceremony, picture, and a researcher must take it with its human aspect, that is, in the way in which it is experienced by the human subjects he investigates' (*ibid.*, 90). According to Znaniecki, human experience was not provided by any universal, objective, featureless space within which other people and things move, including the subject experiencing this space. 'People construct in their experiences innumerable spaces, qualitatively differentiated, limited, indivisible, unstable and positively or negatively appreciated at the same time. The term "space" humanists should use generically, denoting the whole class of these specific and particular spaces' (*ibid.*, 91). Znaniecki proposed to speak rather about spatial values. None of the latter are independent, 'each is a component of a certain aspatial system of values with reference to which such a spatial value acquires a specific meaning and essence. There are a variety of value systems, for example, religious, aesthetic, technical and productive, economic, social, etc.' (*ibid.*, 91).

According to Znaniecki, spatial value acquired a specific meaning with respect to the experience and activity of social group. Such groups possess in the sphere of their collective experience and activity certain spatial values which are treated as a common property of their own, not in a pure economic sense, but with a more general meaning, according to which groups rule these spatial values using them to accomplish certain collective activities [. . .]. Thus for example, for a social group on a national scale, such a spatial value is the territory of the country occupied by members of the group [. . .], for a religious group common spatial values, which are especially claimed to be ruled, are holy (sacred) places, although its property in its eyes is also the entire territory inhabited by coreligionists [. . .], for a productive group, the area under farm or factory, for family its flat, for an association the place of meetings – all these are social values considered as integral components of social group life (*ibid.*, 92).

With the idea of the group spatial value, Znaniecki introduced another concept having a strict spatial connotation. It was the concept of ecological position. As Znaniecki noticed, the group as a ruler of its spatial property (value), was entitled to permit individuals to occupy places within space. Such a right an individual was granted (bestowed) by the group. The spatial position which was acknowledged (admitted) to the individual depended on his or her social role, or on where he or she stood in society. It was this position that Znaniecki termed an ecological one. Ecological position was thus the right to occupy a place within a common spatial property acknowledged to individuals by a group, which corresponded with their social positions, and constituted a part of their social statuses (Znaniecki 1938).

The humanistic approach to the problem of the man–environment relationship was forgotten for a long time, and only recently geographers in Poland rediscovered it and applied it within the conceptual framework of humanistic geography. This is one example when a former idea which existed in a relict form was later revived and employed in different circumstances.

The regional approach

Like in West European geography, the concept of the region and the related regional paradigm developed in Eastern Europe on the basis of the idea of chorology. The latter was the intellectual product of the German school introduced by I. Kant, then applied by C. Ritter in his concept of unity and diversity, and developed in ultimate form by F. Richthofen and A. Hettner. In general, chorology was interpreted as 'the examination of the areal associations of things of diverse origin' (James and Martin 1981, 179).

In East European geography, the concept of region and the regional approach were introduced relatively early. The first was the Czech geographer Koristka who applied the chorological point of view, relying mainly on the ideas of Ritter. Koristka introduced and elaborated the idea of a uniform region, interpreting it as a spatial class of events and phenomena on the face of the earth characterized by a large interclass similarity and at the same time a large diversity with regard to other adjacent spatial groupings of things. He delimited his homogeneous regions within Bohemia and Moravia in 1869, using as criteria the features related to natural conditions as well as the agriculture and forest economy of Czech land (Strida 1961).

Since then the regional paradigm has developed in other countries of the subregion. Three approaches constituted the conceptual content of the paradigm. They emerged chronologically. First, the concept of the uniform region was applied by Koristka; second, there appeared an idea according to which region was interpreted as a human landscape, and third, the concept of the nodal region was introduced into East European geography. These three approaches are presented successively in the remainder of this chapter.

Regions as uniform spatial classes

According to the methodology elaborated at that time in the West (especially in German geography), a uniform region was assumed to be an area of any size presenting some kind of homogeneity from the point of view of the criteria applied to define it. These criteria were formulated for a given purpose, which implied referring to particular groups of items from the whole range of phenomena. The first regional studies were based on criteria of both a natural and an economic character. As agriculture was the prevailing form of human activity in the subregion at that time, the most common was the identification of areas of homogeneity in terms of natural conditions and characteristics describing rural economy. This approach developed particularly well in the area of what later became Czechoslovakia. Strida (1961) presents examples of several large regional studies undertaken there in the modern period. Aside from Czechoslovakia, the regional approach using natural and agricultural criteria developed quite well in Hungary (Bora 1961) and to a lesser degree in Romania (Stan 1961).

As the economies of the countries in the subregion became gradually more diversified and specialized, geographers started to pay more attention to economic characteristics rather than natural features, and more and more economic criteria were applied to delimit uniform regions. The material which was used mainly took the form of statistical data. This data presented the values of certain variables selected as criteria of regionalization. As a result, statistical (economic) regions were identified in the form of spatial classes where the values of the variables had maximum homogeneity. This point of view was first applied in Poland in 1915 and a number of valuable studies developed there later (Dziewonski and Wrobel 1961).

A quite different approach to the problem of the delimitation of economic regions developed in Bulgaria. Here, A. Beshkov considered the territorial differentiation of the economy as the result of the territorial division of labour. As this process was objective, there were various objective combinations of economic activities in different parts of the country. These parts, or regions, were thus real objects, and the task of geographers was not to conceive or create them, as in the case of the statistical approach, but to identify and delimit (Marinov 1961).

Regions as cultural landscapes

Despite a number of studies conducted in the countries of the subregion, the concept of the economic region as a uniform spatial class did not find wider support. Prevailing at that time was the opinion that the basic purpose of geographical studies was to identify areal units that presented a specific synthesis of natural and cultural factors. Such units were known as cultural or human landscapes; the term was taken from the German word *Kulturlanschaft*. The concept of geography as a landscape science was borrowed from the German school, primarily from the works of O. Schluter (Dziewonski 1956).

After Schluter, human landscape was interpreted as the result of a long-lasting interplay between human activity and natural conditions. The landscape took the form of a deeply transformed, humanized fragment of the earth's surface whose content was composed of both natural and man-made objects. The specific features and associations both among objects themselves and with the area gave the latter a distinctive character and distinguished the area from other ones. The task of geographers was to describe this distinctiveness in terms of the landscape morphology.

The cultural landscape was dynamic in nature. Its present physiognomy was the result of changes that had occurred over a long period of time. This implied that in order to understand fully the present morphology it was necessary to study the evolution of the landscape starting from its original form as it existed before changes were introduced through human activity.

Later, another approach developed in East European geography based on the French tradition of human geography with the focus placed on the concept of the *milieux* as the closest, immediate physical setting modified and changed by human activity. After Demangenon (1920), landscape was treated as reflecting the unity of physical and human components constituting a specific equilibrium between the activity of man and natural conditions. The morphology of the landscape reflected a state of such an equilibrium at a particular moment in time. To understand this morphology required going back in time and tracing the changes that brought about its contemporary pattern.

The most common material form in which the idea of the cultural landscape manifested itself in reality was the phenomenon of human settlement. Studies of this phenomenon consisted in describing and explaining the morphology or physiognomy of human habitats. Various features characterizing this morphology were used to identify spatial units which were homogeneous from the point of view of the criteria adopted. Cultural landscapes were thus interpreted as small regions where man-made objects and natural features constituted a specific homogeneity distinguishing these landscapes from their surroundings.

Explanations of human landscape had to discover the causes that created the peculiarities of their physiognomy. There were two models of this explanation. The morphological model elaborated in the German school sought to present the form of a settlement pattern in terms of the factors characteristic of the pattern itself. These were the building material of which habitats were constructed, architectural styles, the ways they were grouped into various spatial forms, etc. The other was the functional model borrowed from French geography. It focused on the relationship between the form of rural habitat and the type of rural economy. This relationship became more obvious when other factors constituting the human *milieu* were taken into account, such as natural features, the cultural characteristics of the population, its demographic attributes and forms of economy and economic development. In both models the stress was placed on a historical analysis of the series of changes in the past that had led to the contemporary form of the cultural landscape.

Studies in settlement geography and cultural landscape played a particular role in East European human geography. In practice, they were an integral part of two paradigms. First, they provided valuable empirical evidence for dealing with the problem of the man–nature relationship. This problem underlay the very idea of the cultural landscape which was interpreted as an association of physical and human factors resulting from the mutual interplay between human activity and natural features. Second, the morphology of the cultural landscape was the subject matter of the regional paradigm. The features of this morphology were the necessary basis for applying this method of regionalization and for identifying landscape regions. This wide empirical significance was the main reason that settlement and cultural landscape studies were the best developed research field in East European human geography. The investigations concerned both urban and rural settlement; the studies of the latter were much more advanced, however, as a rural way of life and related settlement patterns (cultural landscape) predominated all over the subregion.

The largest school of cultural landscape and settlement geography developed at that time in Poland (Romanowski 1964). The leading workers within the field were Potkanski (1922), the originator of the functional approach focusing firmly on historical analysis, as well as Zaborski (1926) and Kielczewska (1931) who developed and enriched the approach. The morphological point of view was initiated by Sawicki (1910) and Pawlowski (1926). The latter contributed much to theoretical considerations on the nature of landscape, especially on the problem of the non-material content of human regions (Pawlowski 1924). Dziewonski (1956, 747) distinguished seven major trends that developed within the field: studies of distribution and structure of population, comparative studies of urban places, urban monographs , investigations of rural settlement, studies of settlement networks, historical geography of settlement systems and methodological works.

The same classification was applicable to other countries of the subregion where different trends developed to a different degree. In Romania, studies concerning rural settlement and settlement networks predominated. In the case of the latter, a valuable functional typology was elaborated by V. Mihailescu, who also originated the studies of functional structure of urban places (Turnock 1984). There were investigations concerning the distribution and structure of population as well as the geography of particular cities (Popp 1938). Original and comprehensive methodological studies were carried out, for example those conducted by Mehedinti (Mihailescu 1977). In Yugoslavia, the form and character of studies in the geography of cultural landscape and settlement were firmly influenced by the assumptions of Cvijic's human geography. Well-developed investigations of landscape regions were carried out by Cvijic's students Milojevic, Jovanovic and Rodovanovic. Rural settlement and settlement networks were another object of analysis. Studies of settlement patterns in rural areas were particularly well developed by Melik and Ilesic, who also contributed much to the geography of urban areas (Thomas 1985) and to population geography (Thomas 1987).

Bulgarian geographers focused mainly on problems of rural settlement, paying much attention to the methodological debate concerning the application of the morphological and the functional approaches. Settlement studies of rural areas were firmly connected with the delimitation of landscape regions, and much interest was devoted to ethnographical, historical and linguistic analysis to identify particularities of national culture and its presence in human landscapes. Aside from settlement studies, investigations were carried out on the ethnic and demographic structure of population and its territorial distribution (Dinev 1966).

The regional approach which developed in Hungarian geography was based on studies of settlement patterns. In keeping with the functional point of view which attracted great interest among researchers, surveys concerning the influence of historical, demographic and economic factors were undertaken to delimit landscape regions in the country (Loczy 1919). A regional study based on the diverse cultural features of the population and types of human habitats was conducted by Teleki (Kish 1987). There were also a few studies dealing with the geography of urban places, in particular the Budapest agglomeration.

Settlement geography in Czechoslovakia was developed by J. Pohl, who conducted a comprehensive study of the rural settlement pattern, its relation to the external environment and a detailed classification (Pohl 1935). In the interwar period a few monographs of larger Czech cities appeared, including Prague.

Economic regions as functional units

The idea of the uniform region was criticized on the grounds of its objective (in-built) inaccuracy. Regardless of how many features demonstrating homogeneity through a region were found, there were always some remaining ones that were not conducive to producing uniformity. On the other hand, it was argued that an area need not necessarily present unity in a taxonomic sense in order to possess a cohesive structure. The latter was the case when different things or phenomena within the region were complementary to one another in a functional sense. Functional ties existed among them which took the form of movements or spatial interactions. There was a specific spatial pattern to this interaction. It was not distributed evenly over the territory of the region, but was subordinated to one or several central points. The networks of interaction within a region had a characteristic order which consisted in centring spatial relations on certain nodes. These, together with the territory connected with them through interaction, constituted what was termed nodal or functional regions.

The idea of the nodal region was first proposed by the Polish economist Wakar (1928) as a reaction to the methodological drawbacks of the concept of the statistical (uniform) region. He maintained that the structure of an economic region should reflect the organization of its social and economic life. As the fundamental feature of this organization he defined the existence of central foci which governed the way in which flows of information, goods and services were spatially distributed over the territory of the region. The role of these foci around which the economic and social life of the region was organized was played by cities. Wakar was the first to identify the relationship between the size of the city on the one hand, and the number of functions provided as well as the size of the area supplied by these functions on the other hand. He applied this formula to divide Poland into functional regions. The regional structure which he obtained was composed of four hierarchical tiers, distinguished from each other in terms of the size of the regions and of the urban places included. Cities occupying higher levels of the hierarchy provided their regions with functions characteristic of lower hierarchical levels, plus some additional kind of supply typical of their level. Wakar was the first, probably together with R. S. Platt (cf. James and Martin 1981, 330), to formulate the major assumptions of central place theory. He, however, neither used the terminology proposed later by W. Christaller nor provided a conceptual systematization of his approach to give it a more consistent or comprehensive form.

A few years later a similar attempt was made by the Estonian geographer E. Kant. He, like Wakar, distinguished in his model four levels of urban hierarchy. Each level consisted of regions surrounding regional centres of similar size and functional structure. Regions of a lower hierarchical order formed, in defined proportions, part of the constitution of regions at a higher level. At the same time, functions performed by smaller centres comprised part of the functional structure of higher-order centres (Gould 1982, 93).

Kant presented his model to the Ministry of Tallin in 1935 as a normative schema for the reform of communal boundaries. According to Buttimer (1987, 75), Kant's proposition assumed 'that administrative structures should reflect the optimal hierarchical ordering of central places, that tax-ation should promote rather than hinder rational development of that hierarchy, and that change should begin with the larger units and only after the overall size and number of regions had been decided should one begin to unify the smaller ones'.

Conclusions

Two different geographies developed in Eastern Europe and Russia during the period called here the pre-socialist era. The term 'geographies' has been used rather than 'human geographies' as the studies pursued for most of the time then were not so much concerned with people as such, rather than with the phenomena of both the physical and the human world. The interest of people to geography appeared later with the emergence of anthropogeography. This was introduced firstly in Russia by Anuchin in the 1880s, and then started to be used in Eastern Europe after Ratzel published his main work at the very end of the last century. The term 'human geography', which appeared at the beginning of the twentieth century in France and replaced the term 'anthropogeography', was practically never employed in Russian geography, nor was it used later in the Soviet Union. In Eastern Europe, on the other hand, it became popular somewhat later, in the interwar period. The relatively short time during which the term was applied, as well as the fact that it was used in part of the region only, have been the main reasons that the term 'geography' has been used in this chapter more frequently.

The periodization of the pre-socialist history of the discipline in the region evaded the classification proposed for western geography by James and Martin (1981). This refers primarily to the history of geography in Russia which developed in a different way as compared with the evolution of the discipline in the rest of Europe (including the eastern part). The most striking characteristic of Russian geography was the appearance of an institutional framework to pursue the discipline in a well-organized way by the late classical period. This, as well as the fact that the modern period was largely the continuation of earlier developments, caused the late classical and modern periods to have been joined into one phase which lasted far longer than the modern period in western geography. In Eastern Europe, on the other hand, the modern period paralleled the developments in the western part of the continent. Newly emerged geographies in East European countries were grounded firmly in models elaborated in Germany and France. The discipline in the region evolved thus in two distinct ways, each with its own duration and individual course of history. The modern period lasted in Eastern Europe and Russia for only a few decades; hence, the term 'pre-socialist' rather than 'modern' has been used to denote the history of the development of the discipline described in this chapter.

In Russia, the major paradigms developed before geography was introduced into universities. All these approaches emerged in the eighteenth century and evolved according to a characteristic causal sequence. At first, the exploration paradigm appeared. It was the product of the contemporary national policy to recognize spatial distribution of natural resources for the needs of economic progress of the country. Information provided by expeditions required classification and generalization, and this stimulated the emergence of the regional paradigm which described and explained the differentiated nature of the national territory. As the differences observed in natural conditions proved to be paralleled by those in human life, another approach developed to study the problem in terms of the relation of man to his physical environment. The new orientations did not appear as competitive approaches. Rather, they complemented earlier paradigms to cope with the problems which were left unsolved. Seeking solutions resulted in the opening up of new fields of enquiry, and the discipline evolved in a branch-like way.

In Eastern Europe, geography started to develop later than in Russia. This development followed to a considerable degree the way in which the discipline evolved in Germany and France. Paradigms that emerged in the subregion concerned the problem of man in association with his physical setting as well as the question of the region and regionalization. As in Russian geography, these were not so much competitive approaches as the orientations which coexisted during the process of the development of the discipline. In both parts of the region, the discipline evolved in a cumulative manner, widening its content and practice with new theoretical and methodological developments. By the end of the period it encompassed a rich mosaic of ideas, concepts and approaches related to many fields of geographical enquiry.

With the beginning of the contemporary period this mosaic was replaced in an unprecedented way by one paradigm only, which seized geography in the region until the end of the 1950s. What happened to the discipline at that time is discussed in the next chapter.

3

The years after the war: the development of economic and regional approaches

The first stage of the process of development of contemporary human geography in Eastern Europe and the USSR covered approximately the years from the end of the 1940s to the end of the 1950s. This phase differed considerably from other stages in the modern and contemporary history of the discipline, just as the decade of the 1950s was clearly distinguishable within the history of the subregion. It was the time when the Stalinist model seized all spheres of life outside the Soviet Union. The academic field was one of the first affected by the new order. In human geography this found its expression in the imposition of a narrow economic paradigm developed earlier in the USSR in the 1930s. In most of the countries in the subregion this paradigm ousted almost entirely the approaches existing there by then. The former tradition was abolished and the process of the economization of the discipline started. Studies dealt primarily with the concept of the economic region and problems of economic regionalization. In the Soviet Union two original and valuable theories emerged which proved to be the only theoretical achievements within the discipline in the region at that time. These theories are presented in the first section of the chapter. In the second section developments in East European human geography are discussed.

The spread of Soviet economic geography

The two theories that developed in Soviet economic geography were both based on the concept of the territorial complex. This concept was applied at first to the problem of the spatial distribution of productive forces, and the theory of territorial production complexes was formulated. The theory is discussed in the first part of this section.

The theory of territorial production complexes

The concept of territorial production complexes grew directly from Lenin's idea of the economic region. The region was defined as a territorially specific combination of economic activities reflecting a certain stage in the spatial division of labour. The concept of the economic region was applied initially in the work on the so-called GOELRO plan (the plan of economic development based on electrification) in the 1920s. This plan was the first attempt (not merely in Soviet Russia) to develop the rational territorial organization of production, or what Lenin named 'a rational location of industry in Russia' (Saushkin 1966, 5). This rationality was considered from the point of view of proximity to raw materials and minimal expenditure of labour within all phases of the production process. The basic assumption of the GOELRO plan was that the driving forces of the national economy should be 'the development and electrification of leading sectors of the economy (the fuel industry, iron–steel, and nonferrous metallurgy) to form the basis for the transformation of other branches of industry' (Saushkin 1966, 7). This process of development was to take place in economic regions whose centres were large regional power stations. Lenin observed such a system in Sweden in 1916 (Saushkin 1973, 254). The combination of branches of production centred around such power stations were to constitute the cores of the economic regions. They were initially termed 'production combines' and later 'territorial production complexes' (Kolosovski 1947).

Work on the regionalization of the country for the purposes of rational economic development was after 1921 conducted under Gosplan (the State Planning Commission) by a special commission on regionalization in Russia. The commission elaborated the basic principles of the methodology of the economic regionalization of the country, presenting the first firmly-stated presumptions of the theory of the economic region as a territorial production complex Saushkin distinguished six such assumptions (1966, 11):

– Each economic region should constitute a large territorial production complex with specialization on a national scale. That complex would include natural conditions; resources; population; historical accumulations, and a material and technical base of production, local consumption and exchange with other regions.

- Regionalization should be based on the energy-economic principle, which means not only that the regional production complex should be based on a system of interconnected powerful regional power stations, but also that maximum labour productivity should be achieved through an optimal combination of productive forces. The energy supply would become the core of the region's economic life.

- Each region should specialize on a national scale in those activities that are favoured to the greatest extent by its natural and manpower resources, its productive potentialities, geographic situation, and transport conditions. Local branches of the economy should develop in each region to the extent that they are needed to ensure the development of the main, national branches of the economy and to supply the needs of the regional population in cheap perishable food and articles.

- It follows that regionalization is also needed for the rationalization of freight hauls through the country. Inter-regional hauls should be limited to those commodities which regions specialize in producing on a national scale. Economic regionalization should serve as the basis for a national network of electrified railways that would handle the major inter-regional hauls. In many cases, these railways in turn would serve as region-forming axes. The ideas of economic regionalization, a system of trunk railroads, and electrification are all interrelated.

- Regionalization is long-term in character, i.e., regional boundaries and the territorial organization of productive forces are designed not only for the present situation, but also for the long-range development of productive forces taking account of the latest trends in science and technology. By looking ahead, regionalization should outpace planning.

- Regionalization should take into account the nationality aspects of economic and cultural development and a number of historical and political considerations, particularly the existence of large region-forming centres with working-class detachments capable of setting an example to the others in fulfilling the economic plan. It is therefore important that economic regionalization be combined with an administrative, political division of the country, and that economic management be combined with political administration.

On the basis of these assumptions a system of twenty-one economic regions was proposed to divide the territory of Soviet Russia. The boundaries of the regions proved not to coincide with those of national minorities, however, which was in part the reason that the Gosplan proposition was rejected by the Party Congress in 1923.

The application of the above assumptions was not a simple task. They were too abstract for practical purposes and, as Kolosovski (1947) claimed, various phenomena were included under the notion of territorial production complexes. They ranged from clusters of plants linked by different relationships, to groups of enterprises located together but not always connected by any linkages. According to Kolosovski, the problem was that the assumptions did not explicitly define which kinds of links among productive units combined them into territorial production complexes. No doubt, an immense variety of connections within every regional economy did not facilitate identifying those constituting the structure of such complexes.

Kolosovski assumed, however, that 'in the whole variety of economic phenomena within the contemporary industrial economy there are some persistently recurring elements. These are the types of production processes. The productive essence of making pig iron is the same in the Donets Basin, in the Urals and in the Kuznets Basin'. A particular type of production process was closely connected with particular kinds of energy and raw materials. Not only was such a leading processing activity invariable, but a certain combination of other production technologies grouped around it was invariable as well. These production activities connected with a particular type of processing activity constituted what Kolosovski termed an energoproductive cycle.

A typical, invariably existing collection of processes, created in a mutual relationship with a leading process for a given type of energy and raw materials is referred here to as an energy-production cycle. [. . .] Thus, the energoproductive cycle is understood as a whole collection of productive processes, successively developing in an economic region of the Soviet Union on the basis of the combination of a particular type of energy and raw materials from extracting and processing raw materials to the production of all the possible types of finished products which can be produced locally by bringing the production nearer to the sources of raw materials and energy, and rationalizing the utilization of all the components of natural resources. [. . .] The cycle should be comprehended as a historical category unfolded in time. (142.)

In other words, the cycle is a group of interrelated economic activities based on the processing of raw materials and utilizing a particular energy source. Kolosovski identified eight different types of production cycles, covering all kinds of goods produced.

As Husinec accurately observed, 'an energy-production cycle was viewed as the "building material" of the territorial production complex [. . .] Energy-production cycles were conceived as a means for analysing the technological structure of geographic territorial production complexes. Kolosovski never mixed his structural–technological chains with their geographic formation, the territorial production complexes' (1976, 554). The main purpose of the cycles method was to classify territorial production complexes. Kolosovski interpreted such a complex as a regional combination of different energy-production cycles. For him, the territorial production complex was 'an economic combination of enterprises in one industrial centre, or within a whole region that produces a given economic effect because of a purposeful (planned) selection of enterprises corresponding to the natural and economic conditions of the region with its transportation and economic-geographical position' (1958). This interpretation was in accord with the spirit of the earlier theoretical assumptions related to the GOELRO plan. For Kolosovski, the complex was the core, or if viewing the economic region as a dynamic phenomenon, the core in the process of region formation. The economic core was what grew around this core in terms of related economic and social phenomena. He never attempted to delimit economic regions. In his work he applied regional divisions as already elaborated. Given such regions, he classified them from the point of view of the character of their cores and the nature of the territorial production complexes on which regional structure was based.

The approaches proposed first in the GOELRO plan and then in the Gosplan project became the beginning of the paradigm which achieved its essential form in the works of Kolosovski. Later, other ideas appeared within the paradigm which did not add much to its essence. They were more modifications of what had been proposed earlier, rather than new theoretical knowledge. The paradigm has dominated Soviet human (economic) geography for a long time since, and even now it still attracts considerable interest among geographers in the former USSR.

The attention paid by economic geographers in the West to the territorial production complex theory is attributable to the similarities and analogies between the notions used in it and certain fundamental concepts in western economic geography. As Lonsdale (1969) suggests, the concept of the territorial production complex was in fact the first attempt at the formulation and practical application of the idea of a nodal region. On the other hand, he shows an analogy between the former and Isard's theory of the industrial complex. Husinec (1976) points out that there are similarities between Kolosovski's formulation of territorial production complexes on various spatial scales – regional, subregional and local – and some concepts of central place theory. He also identifies similarities and differences between concepts in territorial production theory and energy production cycles and basic notions of growth poles – growth centres theory.

Despite its great interest and wide application, the theory of territorial production complexes met with criticism in the Soviet Union, directed mainly at the approach proposed by Kolosovski. Critical remarks concerned firstly the technical character of Kolosovski's argument, and the complete separation of problems related to the social aspects of the phenomena presented. Reservations that appeared later were of a more fundamental character. Lis (1977), for example, pointed out the failure of the theory to consider the economic aspects and consequences of various combinations of inter-industry linkages which were important issues from the point of view of the need for rationality underlying the assumptions of the theory. It can therefore be difficult to define which combination of industries is optimal in a given situation.

The theory of socio-cultural territorial complexes

Kolosovski's idea was not the only one that appeared at that time. In the same year another geographer presented his theory in which he also used the concept of the territorial complex. This geographer was Kabo (1947). He introduced the idea of so-called socio-cultural territorial complexes, basing it, as Kolosovski did with his theory, on the assumptions of historical materialism.

According to Kabo a socio-cultural complex was the subject matter of the subdiscipline in human geography which he called socio-cultural geography. This complex was assumed to be a spatial expression of a wider phenomenon which Kabo considered of great interest to human geographers. This was the phenomenon or rather the process of mutual interplay between society and the environment. The interplay had a dialectical character, in the sense that it conditioned the development of both society and the natural environment. For Kabo, the very society was structured by another interplay. This was the relationship between pro-ductive forces and social relations. Thus, he interpreted the man–environment interdependence in terms of the relationships among three elements: the natural environment, productive forces and social relations.

Relations between people and the natural environment were shaped in the process of social production. Since the latter reflected the unity of productive forces and social relations, the mutual interplay between people and the environment could not exist without relations among people (social relations). While changing, social relations influenced productive forces, thereby affecting the natural environment. At the same time, how-ever, while moulding nature, man transformed the productive forces which shaped social relations. There was a balance between the level of development of productive forces and the state of the natural environment, which was destroyed through the changes in the process of development of productive forces. The latter process at the same time brought about changes in social relations. Thus, the relationship between man and the environment was not a simple relationship. It took place within a particular social formation. The laws of this formation and those of productive forces conditioned human activity in the natural environment. Man might act as a villain or modern capitalist farmer, each time forming a different relationship with his natural environment.

Every natural environment transformed by man reflected major features of a society. In essence, the character of this influence was always conditioned by social relations. The way the society affected the natural environment was governed by the type of social relations (relations of production), but environmental conditions individualized this influence and tended to create different cultural landscapes. Given the same relations of production in a society, different cultural landscapes were produced according to the conditions of the natural environment. The intensity and deepness of the transformation depended on the level of development of productive forces. Landscapes changed slower or faster in accordance with this level.

The key category which Kabo used in his theory was that of way of life. The concept connoted a broad spectrum of phenomena. In general, way of life was defined in terms of both the means of subsistence and how people gained them, and which forms their lives assumed across a wide field of human behaviour and culture. There were two types of factors shaping the ways people lived. Kabo called them primary and secondary factors. The former were the social relations characteristic of a society: the latter, the influence of local environmental conditions. Social relations defined the major principles of a way of life, while environmental conditions provided that way of life with its specific, local colour.

Human behaviour, activities, customs and habits and various aspects of way of life had their specific spatial expression. Similar environmental conditions created similar forms of this expression. Within a territory characteristic of the same environmental conditions originated common patterns of human activity which created what Kabo termed socio-cultural territorial complexes. Thus, a society joined into one whole by the primary features of social relations of production disintegrated with regard to secondary characteristics into socio-cultural complexes on various spatial scales: subnational, regional, subregional, local.

Kabo often termed these complexes socio-territorial groups of people. According to him, socio-cultural geography concerned social and environmental conditions of various types of human activity and forms of life, ways people lived and socio-cultural peculiarities within their spatial dimension, as well as combinations of all these elements characteristic of each separate socio-territorial group of people.

The two approaches – Kolosovski's theory of territorial production complexes and Kabo's idea of socio-cultural territorial complexes (socio-territorial groups of people) – did not compose one coherent theory of human geography, though they were both based on common assumptions of historical materialism. Instead, they were rather theories of two separate subdisciplines in human geography: the former of economic geography, the latter of socio-cultural geography. This division was maintained and even enlarged by contemporary political circumstances. Economic geography, its tasks and methods were seen and judged from the viewpoint of its contribution to the process of the reconstruction of national economy damaged by the war. A significant role in this attitude to the discipline was played by its achievements during the interwar period when it proved to be useful in the work on plans to develop the national economy. This caused economic geography to be firmly supported by political circles, who always had a decisive influence on what occurred in academic life, particularly in the Stalinist era. At the same time, the attempts to develop fields other than economic geography were impossible and even dangerous. That was why Kabo's theory met with severe criticism. His adversaries could not understand the significance of human culture and habits, or such particulars as the sorts of clothing that people wore, or the type of food they ate, when the most important aim was to achieve actual changes in reality by the development of productive forces. As a result, Kabo's approach was rejected as not understandable and unnecessary.

In the 1950s, the only form in which human geography existed in the USSR was economic geography. Traditionally, social problems were included within the category. Thus, geographical branches concerning various aspects of the life of human society such as political geography, urban geography or cultural geography were encompassed by economic geography (Konstantinov 1961). Social aspects were examined as the eventual products of economic conditions and processes. Perhaps the best developed within the discipline was population geography. Phenomena that the branch studied, 'the distribution of population, the character of that distribution, types of populated points, etc. to a considerable extent depend[ed] directly or indirectly upon the productive activity of the people. Hence all (or nearly all) questions of population geography [could] be examined within the framework of economic geography' (Konstantinov 1961, 31).

In 1955, at the Second Congress of the Geographical Society of the USSR, economic geography was defined as a social science concerned with the geographical location of production (meaning the unity of productive forces and productive relationships) and the conditions and characteristics of its development in various countries and regions. Stress was laid on the importance of economic regionalization as significant both for economic planning and for the development of economic geography as a discipline (Saushkin 1966).

Research work in the discipline followed two major trends often termed general and regional. The former dealt with the problems of 'the economic evaluation of the natural conditions and natural resources, the distribution of the productive forces as a whole throughout the country, the geography of population, and the geography of industrial branches of the national economy. [. . .] The latter concerned questions of economic regionalization and the study of the economic geography of separate republics and economic regions of the USSR' (Konstantinov 1961, 32).

According to the cited author, geographers mainly paid attention to the regional approach. 'There is a great multitude of economic geographic works devoted to the republics, economic regions and cities' (Konstantinov 1961, 33). These works dealt not only with the economic structure of regions, but also with more sophisticated problems of economic regionalization in the areas under investigation, mainly using the assumptions of the theory of territorial production complexes (Saushkin 1966, 56). Applying this theory led on to the problems of not only the location of productive forces as a whole, but also the location of individual sectors of the economy. Studies of the development and location of branches of material production developed steadily at the end of the 1950s, and were paralleled by the introduction of new methods of locational analysis.

Studies outside the USSR: the introduction of the regional approach

As stated earlier, the postwar period in East European human geography was until the end of the 1950s characterized by the domination of the Soviet model. The idea of the region and regionalization with regard to the problems of the spatial distribution of productive forces constituted the majority of the theoretical background to the discipline. Geographical research on economic regionalization was, however, not merely a faithful copy of the approach applied in the Soviet Union. It was often based on a similar and even identical theoretical background to that of western human geography, although it differed in terms of the question of the character and role of the economic region. The difference came from the fact that the characteristic aim of East European countries was to create a classless society by means of a planned economy. The socialization of the means of production involved handing the management of productive enterprises over to the state and, subsequently, to smaller territorial administrative units. In consequence, basic administrative divisions became, after a time, administrative and economic divisions, and their economic role steadily increased. The fulfilment of functions and economic tasks by the territorial administrative divisions required that they should be related both to the existing regional structure of the country, and to the processes of its improvement and modification. Current planning regions needed to be shaped by taking into account regions planned for the further future.

Thus, in the countries of the East European subregion there was a vital need to learn about the structure of the national and regional spatial economy and to ascertain the possibilities and suitability of social, economic and technical changes. Consequently the theme of economic regionalization – equally important both for the scientific knowledge of reality, and for the practical needs of social and economic life – appeared in geographical research.

The basic theoretical background against which the studies on regionalization were based was, in the first place, the assumption (borrowed from the Soviet school) about the objective existence of economic regions.

Economic regions as objective entities

The concept of the economic region was applied in East European human geography under the influence of the philosophy elaborated in Soviet geography. According to this philosophy, the term 'economic region' signified a spatial socio-economic grouping which found lasting expression in the economy and investments of a given territory. Each economic region was the result of historical processes; it was changing through time, extending from the past into the future, and its development, similar to the whole socio-economic process, was due to the quantitative and qualitative growth of productive forces (Dziewonski 1967).

The evolution of economic regions was, according to the results of investigations, characterized by the development of greater spatial units with stronger differentiation and closer internal ties of steadily growing economic significance. Geographers shared the common view that the creation of economic regions was connected with and was an expression of the growth of the territorial social division of labour. The logical consequence of such an assumption would be to accept the criteria of economic zones, or zones defined by the types of regional and local economies. In view, however, of the fact that the economic structure was always tied, to a lesser or greater extent, to administrative divisions, and that the organization and development of the regional economy was temporarily the result of the decentralization of the national economy, the problem of nodal regions could not be eliminated from the analysis. Those criteria were, however, quite different. As a result human (economic) geographers were faced with the serious methodical problem of defining their mutual interdependence and hierarchy. The same problem occurred sometimes in a different form, namely in a contradiction between the criteria for specialization of regional production, and those for economic autarchy in the region. Geographers attempted to solve those difficulties by different means. The existing differences in opinions could be assumed as a basis for the classification of several geographical schools and approaches in the countries of the subregion. In spite of unanimous recognition of the basic elements of the theoretical and methodological approach to the problems of regionalization, materials gathered and discussions held testified that there were also some problems omitted or insufficiently discussed.

Regarding the interrelationships between criteria for zonal and nodal structure, or for specialization of production and autarchy in the economy, a group of Polish geographers were of the opinion that differences in existing types of economic structure in a given country were primarily connected with the stage of socio-economic development, but were also related to the geographic environment, as well as to the historical socio-economic development of the region. Thus, in all studies of the contemporary regional structure (or regional division) of a country, it was necessary to include the problems of zonal and nodal structure and to determine their interrelationships, on the basis not of some *a priori* assumptions, but on inductive reasoning. Thus the problem of the typology of economic regions acquired a special significance.

Studies on the formation and development of economic regions carried on in East European countries could be classified according to the directly implied aims of the research, or the applied methods of analysis. Based on the criterion of the aims of the research, it was possible to differentiate the following main types of the research analysis:

- Analyses connected with the intended reform of the administrative and economic divisions; works of such type were carried on in all the countries of the subregion.
- Scientific research connected with the preparation of regional plans which determined trends for the future development of the economy of the country and its regions; works of such type developed in Czechoslovakia, Poland and Romania.
- Analyses carried out for the purposes of operative economic planning;

works of such type were carried out in Bulgaria, Czechoslovakia and (partly) in Poland.
- Special studies aimed at the economic rehabilitation of underdeveloped areas or those with a less developed economy; such work was done in Czechoslovakia and Poland.
- Purely scientific research on the typology of regions and their historical genesis; studies were carried out in Poland.

The dominant element of analyses connected with changes of administrative divisions was, as a rule, localization and accessibility to the main centre (hence the problem of regional nodal structure), although problems dealing with equalization in size (of the area or of the population, or both) of similar administrative units were also considered. In connection with the decentralization of management, steadily increasing attention was paid to economic strength and the balancing of regional income and expenses of a given district (or administrative unit).

Scientific research carried out for regional planning usually involved the preparation of complex analyses, and a tendency to use different methods simultaneously was therefore quite evident. Such studies often evolved into large regional monographs. The important feature of the latter was the tendency to include economic or even econometric calculus based to a great extent on global figures and universal economic indexes. This tendency was typical for analyses carried out for operative planning.

In special studies aimed at the economic rehabilitation of regions which often differed in size and significance, a slightly different method of regional analysis was developed. Rehabilitation of a region required estimates of its reserves and ascertainment of its economic possibilities. Consequently the analyses and appraisal of the basic characteristic features of the geographical environment and the forms of its economic use played an important role in such studies.

Purely scientific research, i.e. theoretical studies dealing, among other things, with the general typology of regions and with their historical genesis, was of a great practical significance. Its development stipulated the improvement of all other types of studies and analyses, and was of a direct use for economic planning. It also involved a tendency to introduce comparative methods, together with extensive economic analyses based on global data, statistical indexes and economic calculus.

A new type of research which was of great theoretical and practical significance for the analysis of economic regions and which dealt with the international social division of labour was initiated by the end of the 1950s.

There were a number of methods, which can be assigned to the following main groups:

- studies of the distribution of the main types of social economy as defined by global economic quantities, the structure of production, services and consumption, as well as by forms of utilization of the geographical environment expressed, first of all, by land utilization;
- studies of territorial productive complexes;
- studies of the distribution, structure and zones of influence of settlements, complexes of settlements and of the settlement network (the formation of nodal regions);
- analyses of the structure and character of boundaries and transit zones (borderlands);
- analyses of the dynamics of change in time and space of specific regions and of their inter-relations and hierarchy;
- analyses of the relations between the economic regions and the economic and administrative divisions, as well as between existing regions and postulated or planned regions;
- studies of inter-regional relations, as expressed by the international or inter-regional social division of labour, economic co-operation and exchange (Dziewonski 1960).

The economic region and its subjective aspects

By the end of the 1950s the theory of the economic region and economic regionalization was increasingly often criticized on the grounds of two main issues. The first issue was the very nature of the economic region, and the second, the status of the theory purporting, according to the Soviet model, to become the only one within human geography, embracing all the problems of the discipline.

Discussion on the nature of the economic region stemmed from the fact that there were two approaches to this concept in the geographical literature. Soviet and some western geographers agreed with the opinion that an economic region was an objective entity; other geographers, mainly in the West, declared for a formal definition of region according to which the region had an empirical content which depended in every case on the particular problem studied, but was expressed only in a specific kind of mutual relationship among various elements of the earth's surface. According to this kind of definition of the region, the term 'economic region' denoted an infinite variety of types of 'regions' constructed by means of any economic criteria.

The concept of the economic region as an objectively existing entity evolved from the observation of transformations occurring in the areal patterns of economic life under the conditions of advancing capitalist economy. Two fundamental aspects of this process were: (1) a progressive specialization of production and a tendency to concentrate population and production in certain areas, and (2) the intensification, within and around these areas, of economic and social interconnections. In the analyses of this process one of these two aspects was particularly accentuated. For a long time, specialization in areas had been the object of research by economists, statisticians and geographers; as a scientific concept aimed at determining the laws of development of this process, this analysis had, for the first time, found its expression in the works of Soviet scientists. However, the development of the concept of the economic region exposed the problem of the interconnections between human activities especially in the domain of production (the territorial division of labour) and the significance of regional focal places (nodality).

This approach, which linked the concept of the economic region with the concept of the market and that of a productive complex, and which pointed out the dynamic character of such areal units, suggested wide perspectives for research; however it also implied new and considerable theoretical difficulties.

These difficulties were generally connected with the double meaning of the concept of economic region: a) its economic productive content, covered by the concept of a territorial productive complex, and b) the territorial organization of the life of the inhabitants of the area and the servicing of their needs. The latter referred to the hierarchically developed system of service centres and transport: the former, to the interconnections between productive units which did not necessarily form a system corresponding to the system of central places.

The growth of industry during the period of developing capitalism, which led to the collapse of the relatively well balanced regional organization of the feudal era, disrupted the connection between both of these and the regional structure. As a consequence not only of the spontaneous development of a capitalist economy and concrete historical facts, but also of the marked differences in economic and technical conditions of marketing various goods, it was difficult to encounter instances of full correspondence amongst various aspects of economic regionalization which would permit an area unequivocally to be termed an economic region. In particular, it was an exceptional instance where this coincidence would apply to the entire hierarchical system of regions of different rank.

According to Wrobel (1960), such a 'material' definition of the economic region does not permit the establishment of a complete division of a country into economic regions because of the overlapping of various areal patterns treated by such definitions as correspond. That was why he proposed not to eliminate from economic geography the concept of the economic region as an objectively existing entity, but to introduce a related, more general and elastic concept of 'economic regional structure'. This would allow for discordance between these two kinds of interconnections and within each component elements. It would also take into account the differentiations between uniform areas on the basis of the kind and degree of economic development, which would be conceived as the background to the evolution of systems of interconnections.

The second basic problem underlying the terminological confusion in discussion about economic regions was, according to Wrobel, the role of institutional factors. The importance of this problem was seen by analysing the Soviet concept of an economic region. 'As an economic region should be distinguished as a specific, as far as possible economically complete area which, owing to the combination of natural features, cultural accumulations of the past, as well as population with its productive abilities, would constitute a well defined unit of the national economy' (Wrobel 1960, 130).

The practical character of this concept was evident in the way it defined the aim of economic regionalization not in terms of scientific description, but as a means of economic control and management. This planning concept of the economic region had been introduced later into Soviet economic geography as its basic theoretical concept.

However some difficulties arose over the meaning of the 'objective existence of the economic region' – another definition generally supported by Soviet geographers. As Wrobel stated, the nature of these difficulties was the following:

if we assume – as Soviet geographers usually do – that an economic region is necessarily an area of economic planning (i.e. if this feature is included explicitly or implicitly in the definition of the economic region) and at the same time, maintain that an area of the country is actually divided into economic regions conceived as objectively existing entities, then there arises a strong, and natural, tendency to identify economic regions with regions of economic planning and administration, in which case the problem of differentiating economic regions ceases to exist as a problem of economic geography. On the other hand, however, if we define economic region purely in terms of distribution and flows – a subject without doubt to be studied and mapped by economic geographers – the fact remains that these distributions and flows in the conditions of the planned economy are strongly influenced and sometimes even directly determined by the institutional factor of existing administrative division. Therefore it is indeed improbable that, even so defined, economic regions will cross-cut the boundaries of administrative regions. Some discordances of areal patterns of various elements of the so-defined economic region and of the pattern of administrative divisions may be rather expected in many cases. In such a case the really significant problem of economico-geographical study would be to analyse the economic regional structure of the area, instead of dividing the area into economic regions. This means, obviously, that not all regions of administration and planning are objectively existing economic regions as defined by economic geography. (Wrobel 1960, 131.)

The other aspect of the theory of the economic region and economic regionalization which was criticized heavily was the assumption about the crucial role of this theory within human geography, and its ability to embrace all the problems of the discipline. According to the Soviet model, human geography was reducible to economic geography. But for many geographers in Eastern Europe the Soviet concept of economic geography separate from human issues in the discipline.

Resulting from the introduction of narrowly-interpreted economic geography into human geography, there was a steadily growing interest in the geography of economic sectors. Economic geographers, although organizing their studies around regions as complexes, were also of the opinion that the best way to examine these complexes was by studying their parts. Most popular were the studies within the field of industrial geography, agricultural geography and transport geography. These were treated as constituting the whole subject of economic geography which in turn was the same as that of human geography. As part of economic geography there existed the geography of population and settlement. This division into sectors facilitated more profound studies of the processes of production and its variation with regard to geographical space. But this 'economic geography by sector' had nothing in common with the peculiarity of the subject matter of population and settlement geography. It was impossible to combine the latter with other specialisms of economic geography owing to this determined one-sided economic view of the phenomena dealing with man and the geographical environment. A new division of human geography was therefore needed into three equivalent subdisciplines whose subject matter should be: (1) population, (2) settlement and (3) production, the last being interpreted as what was of interest to economic geography. This meant that the latter was a part of human geography subordinated to the needs and assumptions of the discipline.

Conclusions

By the end of the 1950s a strong tendency emerged among geographers, primarily those from the East European subregion, to escape the existing economic and regional paradigm and to enrich human geography with social aspects. More and more geographers started to change their focus, to pay more attention to geography outside economic phenomena and processes, and at the same time they expressed the need for specialization in geographical studies. This found its expression in the way human geography was pursued in the next two decades, which is the topic of the next chapter.

4

The search for new ideas

The end of the 1950s and the beginning of the 1960s were marked by
changes of great importance for the development of human geography in
Eastern Europe and the Soviet Union. The changes occurred under the
influence of three different factors. The most important was the impact
of the political factor. The second half of the 1950s was a period of strong
social movements and struggle against the political, social and economic
system created under communism. As a result (in some countries the
struggle assumed the form of deep social upheavals) the Stalin cult was
abolished and the most severe forms of ruling were liberalized. Reforms
were introduced, spreading into many spheres of political, social and economic life. Although the reforms did not alter the essence of the communist
system, they changed considerably many of its aspects.

The reforms reached science, too. In human geography, as in other disciplines, the point of view was rejected according to which the whole
theory, methodology and research practice were subordinated to Stalinist
dogma. Methodological works appeared criticizing the assumptions of
Stalinist economic geography. Perhaps the best known was the book by A.
V. Anuchin entitled *The theoretical foundations of geography*. It was directed
mainly against 'economic determinism' so popular in Stalinist geography,
according to which the natural environment was irrelevant to the process
of socio-economic development. Anuchin proposed a different interpretation of the subject matter of geography. This should be a discipline, he
said, concerning a dialectical interrelationship between the natural environment and man acting within this environment. Social development could
not be considered as isolated from the physical surroundings, and simultaneously, the latter could not be studied without taking human influence
into account (Anuchin 1960, 58).

The work of Anuchin as well as that of Wrobel about the not necessarily
objective nature of the economic region were the most famous in the theo-

retical and methodological field at that time. They appeared in the same year – 1960 – marking the beginning of a new way of viewing the problems of human geography.

The second factor influencing the development of the discipline in both Eastern Europe as well as the Soviet Union was the growth of systematic studies within the regional paradigm. Besides regional studies having a synthesizing character, studies in topical geography began to appear. Their task was to prepare the material for a regional synthesis. By the end of the 1950s, topical geographies had become independent subdisciplines within human geography and presented another strand of development apart from the regional approach. Thus, at the beginning of the 1960s, in connection with the development of topical specialisms, there developed a new paradigm in human geography. Systematic studies in industrial geography, agricultural geography, urban geography and the geography of services completed the regional paradigm.

The third factor having an impact on changes in human geography in the region were the ideas of human geography which developed at that time in the West. These were largely the ideas of positivist geography which reached the region in the middle of the 1960s and developed during the 1970s.

The last two paradigms, that of systematic studies and the positivist paradigm, marked the development of human geography in the region during the 1960s and 1970s. This development is discussed in three sections into which the text below is divided. In the first section the question of systematic studies is outlined. The positivist approach and adaptation of the scientific method are presented in the second section. In the third section, a systems approach is discussed as a specific aspect of the positivist paradigm which met with great interest mainly in the Soviet Union.

The development of systematic studies and the decline of the regional approach

As in the case of western human geography, systematic and topical geographies in the region grew out of the process of preparation of materials for a regional synthesis. These materials were collected mainly from the topical systematic specialisms which complemented regional geography. Such specialisms which provided regional geography with the necessary materials were studies in industrial geography, agricultural geography, population geography, urban geography and the geography of tertiary activities. They were released from their largely subservient relationship to regional geography and produced topical specialisms with their own subject matters and methods of investigation. In East European and Soviet human geography three topical specialisms played a particular role in the discipline's development. These were industrial geography, agricultural geography and the geography of settlement and population.

Industrial geography

Theoretical and methodological development in industrial geography both in Eastern Europe and the USSR related mainly to the problems of location theory. As earlier stated, Soviet geographers developed the concept of the territorial production complex and within its framework they solved major problems of industrial location. In Eastern Europe, this concept was used far less intensively than in the Soviet Union. Here, geographers took inspiration rather from the work of western geographers, particularly the German creators of location theory (Dziewoński 1961). However, both in the USSR and Eastern Europe the methodology used was based not only on the classic models of spatial location; it was also closely related to the issue of how to plan patterns of industrial location. This was mainly because location was strictly controlled and directed according to specific guiding principles. The underlying assumption was to create a socio-economic system in space where there were no disproportions between regions. The so-called socialist location policy sought to avoid these disproportions by paying most attention, from the very beginning, to the correct location of industry as the decisive element in the development of the whole national economy (Secomski 1974).

The approach to location applied in the region replaced the individual profit motive, as in western methodology, with the state's aim of raising production and income to achieve higher, more equal living standards for all everywhere. New industrial development played a key structural and spatial role in this. Maximum social and economic benefit was required of every project. This involved a complex planning approach in order to dovetail plant location into the whole system of spatial linkages between a given plant and other industries, settlements, transport facilities, and land uses, with one eye also on local, regional and national repercussions. Long-term plans and projections of future economic and social trends created a higher degree of certainty, permitting comparative analyses of national, regional and local needs and potentialities. Such analysis created opportunities for a wider choice of location alternatives that permitted more flexible distribution of industry.

According to location theory predominating in human geography in the East European–Soviet region, nine principles of location were mostly analysed and applied. First, industries should be located near to the sources of the raw materials and fuel they used. The aim was to minimize the consumption of labour power. This thought was stimulated by the ideas of Weber, although Lenin had arrived earlier at a similar conclusion independently (Lenin 1918).

Second, industries should be located near to the markets where their products were consumed. This is also, according to the Weberian model, to minimize the transport involved from processing the raw materials through all subsequent semi-finishing stages, through to the marketing of the finished product. Two circumstances reinforced the Weberian model, however. On the one hand, planners largely ignored demand functions and stressed production functions; on the other hand, fixed or manipulated prices, planned demand for capital goods, the limited influence of consumer demand upon the production of consumer goods and the lack of competition encouraged planners to ignore the question of plant location to command the best spatial sales area as a means of maximizing profit (Probst 1972).

The two principles hinted at the clear division between material – and market-oriented industries; yet spatially, the two may be linked, for consumption increased (in mining, fuel and power) as a result of industrialization and the growth of population, while the high level of production (in market areas) made it possible to discover and exploit more efficiently even the second-rate raw materials and fuels. The bases of industrial complexes or agglomerations emerged, but the social frictions of overcrowding, commuting, and housing either encouraged the dispersal of interrelated industries within a growing industrial area, or prohibited new location in inherited capitalist agglomerations (Probst 1972).

These considerations operated within the constraints of the third principle: to locate plants to achieve an even distribution of industry. An even distribution was not meant to imply some standard ratio of industrial employment to area or to population, although it could be understood as that level of industrial development which, combined with other productive activities, ensured equal incomes per head of population over the whole country in the long run. Since incomes were usually unequal, this principle involved the policy of developing backward areas by directing to them proportionately more new industrial capacity than the national average. Priority was given to locating those industries in backward areas that could process materials and energy resources locally and employed much labour.

The importance of developing backward areas was often overemphasized. In reality the principle was to ensure that the development of production in one area would not hinder that in other areas. Some geographers modified this rather vague notion, stressing that the principle required the provision of equal possibilities and opportunities for social and economic development in all parts of the country and giving similar living standards (Bora 1976, Dziewoński 1972). A very long time was necessary to achieve this. In fact, industrial growth was planned for all regions, including the most developed, to supply capital equipment for factories being constructed in the backward areas in exchange for materials and manufactures lacking elsewhere. Nevertheless, the model involved the progressive dispersal of plants to all regions (defined often as territorial administrative areas) of the country, and within each region to both the larger and the smaller towns. It also involved balanced industrial employment for both men and women locally, and balanced regional development in stressing variety as well as some degree of specialization, often around some heavy industrial core area (Probst 1972).

Few principles were stressed as much as this one in development plans. Undoubtedly greater industrial dispersion had resulted, but it was difficult to discern which motive was decisive in each case. More important, the ambiguity and vagueness of the principle virtually gave planners a free hand in choosing locations, particularly for those industries not tied closely to sources of weight-losing materials.

The fourth principle was that industries should be allocated inter-regionally in such a manner as to develop regional specialization according to regional natural resource endowment.

According to the fifth principle, industries should be allocated inter-regionally to achieve greater regional self-sufficiency with respect to regional market needs. In effect, the latter two were restatements of principles one and two, but cast within a regional framework for which the degrees of specialization and of self-sufficiency respectively might be expressed in tables of input–output and inter-industry relations. Distance and transport were far less serious cost factors in Eastern Europe than in the Soviet Union. However, regional specialization and self-sufficiency had major implications for the East European countries within the context of COMECON.

The sixth principle stated that industry should be located so as to advance the economic and cultural development of all regions inhabited by national minorities. This principle was originated by Lenin, who believed that the economic dichotomy between industrial regions and those localized on the periphery was unhealthy to political, social and economic viability in the Soviet Union. Backward regions inhabited by ethnic minorities had to be industrialized. This principle was very relevant in Yugoslavia and Romania. In other countries where the regional ethno-economic problem did not exist, there was the equivalent idea of developing the backward regions at a faster rate than the developed regions. In practice the absence of national minority interests in these states encouraged the supremacy of homogeneous national allocational aspects of economic choice to achieve most rapid overall growth; the deliberate development of backward areas in Poland and Hungary was thus of subordinate importance (Kukliński 1967).

What strategies were, or had been, applied in attempts to industrialize underdeveloped regions in the European socialist republics? Basically, there were three:

- where natural resources were available locally, priority investment went into the development of metallurgy, power and chemicals;
- where natural resources were lacking, heavy industries were constructed if transport access to imported materials was potentially good;
- where neither raw materials for heavy industry nor satisfactory transport links with other regions existed, attempts were made to introduce labour-intensive industries which manufactured high-value products.

According to the seventh principle, industrial location policy should eliminate economic and social differences between town and country, chiefly by greater interdependence between agirculture and industry, the one supplying raw materials for processing, the other the capital goods for raising agricultural productivity. This could lead to the development of processing industries in many rural settlements and of agricultural producers' goods in more central nodes.

The eighth principle was that of dispersing plants in the interests of security and national defence.

The ninth principle stated that industrial choices should facilitate the international division of labour within COMECON, i.e. there should be greater national industrial specialization in accordance with natural and human resource potentials, and hence greater international economic interdependence. However, four factors operated to restrain the emergence of highly specialized industrial centres within COMECON. Less developed nations, for example Romania, resisted specialization in the primary processing of varied minerals and insisted on developing manufacturing to reduce their historical legacy of backwardness. Conversely, more developed states were reluctant to help eliminate international economic disparities by subsidizing modern factory construction in other less developed states, since this might erode their long-term competitive ability. Moreover, fear of losing political sovereignty to supra-nationality overrode any advantages of production in large-scale plants. Finally, no country was willing, either for economic or ideological reasons, to admit industrial obsolescence since this would undermine confidence in planning (Kaser 1967).

Agricultural geography

Agricultural geography developed first of all in Eastern Europe. One can distinguish three approaches within the field: land use geography; socio-economic and social geography, and the crop and commodity approach.

There were a number of attempts at land use surveying in Eastern Europe including those by the Bulgarians, the Romanians and the Poles. In Poland, J. Kostrowicki adapted the British land use survey to the native conditions of Poland, modified it through field experience in other countries of the subregion, and produced a volume of work which appeared much superior to its British predecessor in analytical power. Besides the land use maps, the survey considered the state of land improvement, field fragmentation, ownership fragmentation and land tenure conditions (Kostrowicki 1966).

The task of providing a scientific topology of the agricultural systems never succeeded, however, reflecting no doubt the forbidding complexity of agriculture. The problem was to devise an agricultural topology which would be transferable in time and space. It was thus logical that geographers, after concerning themselves with land use surveying, turned to the problem of developing a typology.

One approach to a typology was by means of regionalization. Regionalization was a necessary part of any typology but could not precede it. For this reason the definitions of the various agricultural regions were not definitions of types of agriculture, but agricultural regions usually delimited with a great deal of intuition and common sense. At the other end of the scale there were studies of individual farms or of very small areas, studies which were capable of fully describing the farm operations but incapable of correlation into valid syntheses of larger regions.

Geographers were aware that agriculture was not the business of using the land, but rather that of obtaining a livelihood from the land. That meant that the agricultural type was conditioned by the socio-economic forces acting upon an environment and not by a form of land use. Investigations included such socio-economic factors as ownership, management, labour supply, size of holdings and share of agriculture in the total employment. Among the agricultural factors the study considered land fragmentation and patterns of land use, quality of land, water and climate management, biological control, cropping systems, husbandry techniques and the livestock-to-land ratio. The study also considered labour intensity and the aggregate intensity of agriculture. Production characteristics formed a whole sector of factors considered in typology. These characteristics were land productivity, capital productivity, degree of commercialization, level of communication, agricultural orientation and specialization. This mainly Poland-based survey and potential typology was then expanded and modified to encompass all of the East European subregion. This tested the survey under far greater variations of physical environment, economic development and social conditions. On the basis of such work, agricultural geographers, mainly in Poland, proposed and applied the typology of agriculture for the area (Kostrowicki 1965).

Another approach to agricultural geography and topology was the socio-economic orientation advocated most strongly by the Hungarian geographer, Enyedi. His main idea was that social aspects played a fundamental role in agricultural typology and served as a starting point for it. The same point of view was proposed by the Russian geographer, Mukomiel.

In his book on the agriculture of the world, Enyedi (1967) pointed out that land use alone would not lead to understanding, and he then proceeded deeper into the analysis of social background and economic conditions. He called his types of agriculture 'social types' and based them on 'socio-economic motives'. However, he became too deeply involved in the 'social' aspect at the expense of the 'economic'. The economic factor was characteristically relegated to the position of being merely a social policy, reflecting social conditions and not any economic forces. Using his typology, Enyedi distinguished three agricultural regions within Eastern Europe. Albania, Bulgaria and Romania were considered to resemble the Soviet subtype since collectivization occurred in them before any extensive industrial development. East Germany, Czechoslovakia and Hungary were the second group. Here collectivization occurred when the economy was already well developed. Agriculture was modern not only in social, but also in economic and technological terms. Poland and Yugoslavia, where private farming still prevailed and socialism took on peculiar forms, were placed in the third group.

If the land use approach can be traced to British and then Polish efforts, then the crop and commodity approach can be credited to the Russians. In their typology, the Russians relied mainly on the recognition of specialization – for example, defining the principal crops – and concentration – defining which were the crops on which most of the inputs were concentrated. The measurement of specialization was through the structure of either total production, or that of market production. The unit of measure was either the state commodity price or a conventional (grain or livestock) unit equivalent (Basuk 1962).

Geography of population and settlements

The geography of population and settlements as a separate discipline developed in the East European–Soviet region after World War Two. The growth of the discipline may be partly attributed to the growing quantity and quality of available statistics, but it was mainly the growing awareness of social and demographic changes, and the reconstruction and planning of towns and villages, that prompted geographers to direct more of their time and energy to studying these topics. At this time geographers in Eastern Europe were exposed to the influence of Soviet geography and were adopting the Marxist approach, and development in the East European subregion was similar to that in the Soviet Union.

In all countries of this area the geography of population and settlement was considered a part of economic geography. The latter term referred to all human aspects of geography, and in a sense could be considered an equivalent of human geography as it was understood in Western Europe and North America. Even in Soviet geography, where the term economic geography was first adopted in that broad sense, the awareness persisted that some aspects of the geographic study of population could not be explained in economic terms only.

Discussion of the theoretical aspects of geography, and the geography of population in particular, did not generate as much interest in Eastern Europe as it did among Soviet geographers, and the number of theoretical studies and statements is rather limited. In the Soviet Union the geography of population was separate from settlement geography. Pokshishevski (1964), for example, defined the geography of population as a socio-geographic discipline which studied population in the process of social reproduction from the point of view of the growth and structure of the population with regard to spatial factors. In Poland, where theoretical discussion was perhaps more advanced than in other countries of Eastern Europe, the separation of population and settlement geography was also accepted. Kosiński (1967) defined population geography as a separate branch of economic geography, which studied and interpreted the spatial aspects of demographic facts and processes that vary in time and space on the earth's surface.

As far as research topics were concerned, there was a great similarity among scholars from different countries, who concentrated their interests on population distribution, density, composition and changes. The spatial aspect was considered to be a *signum specificum* of geographical study, and consequently demographic cartography was normally included in population geography.

Although the research interest and scholarly contributions of geographers in the East European–Soviet region into the geography of population and settlement were very uneven, certain groups of topics can be distinguished. These were population monographs, population distribution and density, the structure of population, population change, commuting, settlement networks, urban studies and rural settlement.

Population monographs dealt with a general description of the demographic situation of the area in the various countries and regions. Some demographic discussions were very extensive, as in the monographs on Hungary (Pecsi and Sarfalvi 1964). The chapters on population and settlements were also quite exhaustive in the monographs on Romania (Gherasimov 1960), Bulgaria (Beshkov and Valev 1961), Poland (Berezowski 1969) and Yugoslavia (Blaskovic 1967), and large parts of the great regional monographs dealt with demography. Two examples were the monographs on the Bialystok *voivodship* (Kostrowicki 1967) and on the East Slovakian mining and industrial region (Ivanicka 1964). Both summarized the results of extensive research done by geographers in connection with regional plans prepared for these areas.

Various aspects of the demographic and/or settlement pattern were discussed in demographic monographs on countries or smaller areas. The list of monographs, which varied both in size and in quality, is long, and only a few of the more valuable ones can be cited here, for example the monograph by Buga (1967) on Romania, Dinev and Velchev (1965) on Bulgaria and Friganovic (1962) on Yugoslavia. Some regional descriptions bore witness to the long-standing tradition of the French regional school (especially in Romania and Yugoslavia). In others the applied approach was more apparent. Geographical traditions emphasized a holistic approach to the topics studied. Consequently the comprehensive monographs tended to be considered the most 'geographic'. There was even a tendency to identify the discipline of population geography with a general description of demographic phenomena of a particular area, but this narrow approach was not accepted.

Population distribution and density were the topics which were traditionally studied by geographers and the relevant literature was fairly extensive. There were numerous studies based upon maps of population distribution and density. In Poland, an attempt was made to use the dot map of population distribution as a basis for a density map, whereby the abstract hexagonal units were applied. The most extensive analyses of changes in the distribution of population were published by Haufler (1967) for Czechoslovakia, and by Dziewoński and Kosiński (1965) for Poland. The latter appeared as the first volume of a large demographic monograph on Poland which was prepared by different authors. In both books, discussion was not limited to the classical aspects of population distribution alone, but also included centrographic measures and measures of population potential and concentration.

The Lorenz curve was used by Polish geographers in the study of population concentration in Poland and other countries. Changes in population potential in Poland were discussed. Hungarian demographers also became interested in population distribution, and a new approach involving mathematical procedures was presented by Tekse (1965). Staszewski (1960) published studies of population distribution in relation to altitude, coastline and climatic zones.

The structure and characteristics of population attracted geographers less than in the past. This was particularly true of ethnic and linguistic structure. The complex ethnic patterns in the region between the wars were very often analysed by geographers from different countries. After World War Two they were usually discussed in general monographs, but only rarely did they generate separate studies. This might be due to the fact that the ethnic structure was substantially simplified, and the proportion of ethnic minorities had declined from about 24 per cent before World War Two to about 7 per cent after the war. Another factor was the decline of interest in political geography. It was often within the context of the latter that ethnic topics were discussed. On the other hand, Soviet publications in the field of ethnic geography, and in particular the well-known *Atlas narodov mira*, generated some general studies (Piasecki 1964).

The biological structure of population was discussed only infrequently. It was considered in studies of labour balance-sheets carried on in Sofia University and commissioned by government agencies. Some publications from Poland and Hungary can also be mentioned. Social and occupational structure and changes caused by increasing urbanization and industrialization became more attractive for geographers in recent times. The impact of urbanization was studied in Poland, and there was a Yugoslav study on Nikšić (Krivokapić 1966). Sarfalvi (1965) studied social stratification in Hungary, and later attempted to apply his concepts to Europe. Leonhard-Migaczowa (1965) suggested using the structures of population as a basic criterion for defining demographic regions. Studies of the socio-economic characteristics of the population transcended the boundaries of population geography and were examples of more comprehensive research into social geography which was not then recognized as a separate field.

Population change, that is, dynamic aspects of demographic phenomena, were considered in several studies dealing with the distribution or structure of population. World War Two accounted for the involuntary migration of more than 25 million people in Eastern Europe alone. The largest, partly caused by territorial shifts, occurred in Poland. A number of geographical studies discussed the resettlement of newly-acquired territories or areas depopulated as a result of the war (Kosiński 1963, Maryanski 1963). Similar studies, although not as numerous as in Poland, were undertaken by Czechoslovak and Yugoslav geographers. These were rather detailed investigations and there were no general syntheses.

In the postwar years, migration in the region was very high as a result of intensive industrialization and urbanization. Rural–urban migration and its consequences was studied by different authors. Their studies ranged from the local to the international. In Hungary, the emphasis was on the impact of migration upon rural populations; in Czechoslovakia, on urban migration fields; in Yugoslavia and Romania, on seasonal migrations, and in Poland, on inter-regional migrations.

Population growth and its components were studied in Romania, and in particular in Poland. Perhaps the most interesting studies of natural growth were done by Witthauer (1967), who suggested new methods to study demographic transition. In migrational studies the descriptive approach clearly dominated. This was partly justified by the fact that several great migrations were caused by wars and territorial shifts. However, rural–urban migrations increasingly reflected 'normal' processes of urbanization, and models could be developed to explain or predict them.

Studies on *commuting* were published in Poland and Czechoslovakia, where the relationship between commuting and population density was also studied (Lijewski 1967, Macka 1964). Articles published on other countries of the region were limited to small areas. Two Polish scholars attempted to apply the input–output technique to studies of commuting (Bartosiewiczowa and Czarniecka 1968).

Studies dealing with the *settlement network*, including both rural and urban centers, were mainly concerned with central places, types of communities, and the ranking of settlements. In the early postwar years there was some critical discussion of Christaller's theory, and several studies on that subject were published later, especially in Poland and Hungary (Kania 1963, Boros 1967). Kania published a study based upon German data. She found that the settlement network in part of Silesia was to be adjusted according to central place theory, and she was able to reconstruct the map of villages selected by Nazi regional planners for development as prospective central places. In Czechoslovakia, centrality was investigated in connection with the reform of administrative divisions, and the desire to concentrate investment in administrative centres (Culik 1966). Classifications of communities based upon social, demographic, and economic criteria were published in Yugoslavia (Crkvencic 1966). In Poland the rank-size rule was applied by Kania (1966) to all the settlements of a region.

Zagożdżon (1964) studied the spatial links and groupings of settlements, their patterns and components, and suggested a typology of the existing complexes.

Many *urban studies* were of a general character and described the urban development of a country, the growth of its urban population, and changes in the urban network. Similarly, quite a number of regional urban monographs described aspects of urban development in a given area. The number of monographs on individual cities was also large. Many were commissioned by regional or urban planning agencies. As in other areas of the world, urbanization of the region led to increasing metropolization, but there were surprisingly few studies of metropolitan areas. Some articles appeared in Czechoslovakia, Poland, Romania and the USSR.

Far-reaching changes in the economic bases of small towns, and the decline of many, directed the attention of some geographers, especially in Poland, to the crisis of small towns and possibilities of their economic stimulation. The functional approach was very popular among geographers in Eastern Europe after World War Two, and a large number of studies dealt with the economic bases and functional classification of towns. Although the occupational structure of the population was usually the basic criterion in this type of study, additional criteria such as size and growth of population or the origins of towns were also sometimes taken into consideration. A comprehensive discussion of the development of the concept of the economic bases of towns was given by Dziewoński (1967).

Studies of central places developed rather slowly, partly as a result of sharp criticism of Christaller's concepts in the 1950s. However, there was growing interest, especially in Hungary (Beluszky 1966). The influence of urban centres upon the surrounding area attracted many geographers, and there were many studies of urban hinterlands. Special emphasis was placed upon educational facilities and their influence.

Surprisingly little attention was given to the spatial structure of cities and urban land use. Perhaps it was a reaction against the physiognomic approach prevalent before the Second World War. Nevertheless, the conceptual framework was provided by Dziewoński (1964), who suggested that the classification of towns should not be limited to socio-economic criteria, but that it should also take into account 'material' forms such as the territory of a town, its pattern of development and manner of utilization. The starting point for a morphological classification of towns was, as far as Dziewoński was concerned:

- a definition of the magnitude and complexity of the spatial pattern of the town;

- the determination of the most important constituents of the spatial pattern and especially of its predominant elements;
- the interrelationship of the elements;
- the relation of the spatial pattern to its physical environment;
- the character of its growth within the territory occupied.

However, no empirical studies followed Dziewoński's concept. In Czechoslovakia Hursky (1962) studied the territorial development of urban areas. An ecological structure of Prague was made by Murdych (1965).

Generally speaking, central place theory, which developed as a central theoretical concept of urban geography in the West, failed to perform the same function in the East European–Soviet region. This can partly be explained by the fact that it represented a model which was criticized for its abstractness. The fact that the concept was not unpopular among Nazi planners did not encourage scholars in this part of the world to accept it. The concept of economic base became most popular among urban geographers in the region, and was used both for analyzing the existing situation and for predicting future trends.

The great interest which geographers in the region had in the problem of *rural settlement* came from the fact that the rural population always accounted for a large share of the total population of the countries of the region. The rate of change and the kind of problems encountered were well illustrated by Velchev (1967), who studied the rural population of Bulgaria in the postwar years. The long tradition of research into the origins and spatial structure of rural settlements was continuing but, contrary to earlier studies, there was a strong tendency to consider the spatial aspects in relation to the functions of settlements, and to study the layout of rural settlements together with the field patterns. Most of those studies belonged, in fact, to historical geography. The specific character of Hungarian problems was reflected in the emphasis on agricultural towns and dispersed settlements which had developed when the plains, depopulated during the Turkish invasion and control, were resettled (Tajti 1970).

Another traditional approach – the study of rural settlements in relation to the physical environment – was applied very rarely. On the other hand, a growing body of literature represented a more applied approach. It was found mainly in studies of the dispersion of rural settlements and possible ways of rearranging them. Similarly, a practical aspect was present in a Czech study on the accessibility of rural settlements (Vlcek 1964) and a settlement study of Hungary (Beluszky 1965). There were also studies of transitional settlements whose role was increasing in the region. Another category consisted of studies describing different aspects of rural settlements of a particular area, which were especially popular in Romania and

Yugoslavia. In Romania, place-names were studied wit
of settlements. In other countries, toponomy develo
discipline, although sometimes closely connected with

Human geography as a spatial science: the ac
scientific method

The end of the 1950s and the beginning of the 196
western human geography by a stronger and stronger
hitherto existing idiographic methods of pursuing the
with unique places, according to a regional paradigm,
effective way of progressing human geography and sor
geographers propagated widening the methodology
approach. This had to consist in the development of
tion of quantitative methods and focusing on laws
(Ackerman 1958).

At the beginning of the 1960s, Burton (1963) claim
tive revolution occurred in geography. The positivi
which originated in the United States in the second half
Western Europe by the early 1960s. The method was
ern Europe and the Soviet Union during the second h
the first country in which the method met with wide
The reason was mainly political. Contrary to the o
region, Poland was the only one where scholars had
abroad and contact people from the West. Many Po
visited western universities and came back equippe
ideas and experience which they had gained during

The quantitative and theoretical revolution
Poland and the USSR. Most of the conceptual work
done in the region during the 1960s and 1970s
countries.

The process which helped the advance of the p
the strengthening of systematic and topical ge
released from a largely subservient relationship to
attempts to develop laws and theories of spatial pat
various kinds for illumination, and by applying matl
statistical procedures to facilitate the search for g

The changes in the process of pursuing human
European–Soviet region were most visible with
methodological field. Chojnicki and Dziewoński
four approaches within the theoretical field: (1) t

use and types of agricultural economy. Toge
location, they produced a relatively wide
in Hungarian and Polish economic geogra

In the geography of service systems o
attempts to produce a separate theory of
link service networks with social changes
Also, the time was right for a more inte
activities that were more specialized in char
systems, services) through the theory
underlying concepts.

The second group consisted of *theories of*
and of settlement networks and systems. Althou
was a classic tool organizing the research
help the development of suitable theories
concept formed a basis for formulating
approaches of a descriptive rather than a th
influence of general location theory and mod
attempts emerged to formulate a theory de
nodal region in terms of the openness and c
economic activity. The most developed w
regional development. On the one hand, then
production complexes applied mainly in th
hand, there was the theory of functional urban
of the job market and its closedness, wh
Anglo-American literature.

The theory of territorial production co
vast areas with extensive economies which w
intensive investment and acceleration of eco
functional urban regions was applied to bette
integrated economies in respect of the transpor

Apart from the above-mentioned concept
opment emerged which took the form of
regional economies, often of a normative and
enabled the planning of regional developmer
interregional disparities. These theories were
tigating the spatial economy, so they served

The theory of settlement networks app
Soviet region developed on the basis of a
advanced of which was Christaller's central
the theory of functional structure and econom
for many practical and empirical solutions w
system. These attempts did not, however, form

to construct an overall theory of the settlement system. Consequently, they did not give a satisfactory interpretation or explanation of changes within the settlement network. One of the problems which did not find its solution was that of the hierarchy of settlement units. In reality, this hierarchy was not as explicit a structure as was assumed in the study.

In the research work on settlement networks in the 1970s, a new approach appeared which described these networks in terms of systems theory. According to this theory, a settlement network was described as a settlement system, and its evolution was modelled using the assumptions of the systems approach. This widened the study to include normative and optimizing aspects which brought the investigations closer to planning practice.

The third group consisted of *theories of population distribution and migration.* Their development had an interdisciplinary character, especially with regard to migration. In the last field, there were many concepts and approaches applied which described and explained various forms of migration movements. Among them the most important roles were played by gravity models and models using the assumptions of behavioural geography.

Theoretical problems of the human environment constituted the fourth group of theories developed in human geography in the East European–Soviet region. For the development of the discipline the question of man and the relation of his economy to the natural environment was a leading one which ensured the unity of geography and linked together physical and economic geography. Paradoxically, this task was performed not only by geography, but also by other social, economic, natural and technical disciplines. Among the main achievements were ecological studies and those related to modelling environmental resources and their utilization. In general, however, there was a lack of an integrated theoretical approach and of terminological order. Such basic notions as the human environment, the natural environment, the physical environment, the geographical environment and others were not explicitly defined. The concepts used were mainly attempts to rationalize individual or group attitudes, or opinions based not so much on a critical analysis of reality, as on emotions and feelings.

Apart from in the theoretical field, changes related to the adoption of the positivist paradigm also took place within the methodological field. The deep changes which occurred within the field included both the so-called quantitative revolution, that is, the application of mathematics to geography, and the investigation of qualitative characteristics and relations.

At the beginning of the application of mathematical methods geographers were fascinated with discovering various analytical possibilities given them by quantification. Later, this fascination was replaced by more critical striving to use the methods on those problems which gave the most explicit scientific effect. The process of quantification of the discipline took place in various stages.

At the first stage of collecting and processing information, it was of great importance to develop computer cartography to transform empirical data into a cartographic form. The application of methods of multiple factor analysis was also important. This provided a successful analysis of large quantities of data presenting a differentiated structure. The procedures enabled the development of various typological approaches with regard to social and economic spatial patterns. A fundamental turn occurred at the stage of formulation of regularities and generalizations, thanks to the development of methods of statistical verification and the verification of hypotheses. There emerged various types of mathematical models dealing with interaction in socio-economic space which caused a genuine explosion of studies employing econometric methods. An important influence of mathematical methods was on the process of theory construction. These methods became a tool for concretizing general concepts and notions, thereby confronting theory with the reality. At the same time the application of optimizing methods permitted the solution of planning problems within the geographical research field.

The systems approach and its applications

The systems approach was met with great interest, mainly in the USSR where it was applied primarily to so-called territorial systems. With the beginning of the 1970s the concept of the territorial system became the basic one in the theory and methodology of Soviet human geography, presenting at the same time the fundamental subject matter of the discipline.

A territorial system was defined as a set of elements linked by relationships among these elements constituting a certain functional whole. The links in the territorial systems were characterized by their variety; they dealt with the natural environment, production and society. These links were typical not only of the elements within the territorial system; through the process of system development and evolution there existed a variety of relations among territorial systems themselves (Blazhko 1976).

Territorial systems were clearly differentiated from systems of other types, for example, economic and technical. Their distinguishing feature was that their elements were obligatorily 'attached' to a given territory. This meant that geographical location was distinguished as one of the parameters which permitted the analysis of relations among localized elements in the search for optimization of these locations.

Territorial systems were always very complex, that is, they included large numbers of elements and links among these elements. The elements and the links joining them were distinguished by their variety. For example, in the system of the territorial production complex, the role of elements was played by particular enterprises. Among them there were different firms presenting various profiles and specializations, agricultural and transport organizations, educational institutions of different types and levels, market-supporting firms, and so on. They differed one from another from the point of view of the number of employees, the purposes of their activity, their principles of spatial organization and indexes characterizing their outputs. The links in such systems were even more complicated. In the territorial production complexes, vertical and horizontal links usually developed, mostly of a technological and controlling type, concerning the supply and servicing population, the distribution of resources and the flow of information. These links were constant, or changed with time, playing varying roles in the process of forming the wholeness of the system (Saushkin and Smirnov 1968). A peculiar feature of the territorial system was its dynamic nature, that is, the system's state and structure was capable of changing with time.

The first step in studying territorial systems was to delimit their elements. Which components of the system should be treated as its elements depended on the purpose of the study and the degree of disaggregation of the system's structure. The structure of an element of the system should not, however, be examined in detail. Rather, its features should be investigated which had an influence on the relationships among other elements, or on the character of the system as a whole (Blazhko 1976).

One of the problems studied by Soviet geographers was whether a territorial system had one or many structures, defining the latter as a specific way in which elements and links constituted a particular construction. In fact, every system had one, defined structure characteristic only of it. The point was, however, that there were a number of models, each one mapping this structure from a different point of view. Consequently, while describing various aspects of the structure of the territorial system, they were termed the 'structures' for short as well, for example, an economic structure, a hierarchical structure, a social structure, and so on (Maiminas 1971).

Territorial systems had a number of structural characteristics; some, however, were distinguished by certain particularly important characteristics which were necessary in order to recognize the nature of the systems. Two structural characteristics were identified and applied in the study of these systems: that dealing with the nature of elements of the system, and that dealing with the nature of the relationships in the system. Investigating the former was impossible without examining the latter; in practice, the features of elements were analysed first, and then the study of the links took place. The last was more complex, however, thanks to their extremely differentiated nature. Links in a territorial system were formed as a result of the operation of its elements. An important problem while studying territorial systems was that of the classification of the relationships in the systems. Two types of links were distinguished: inflexible and flexible. The flexible relationships were those which did not change in a particular state of the system's behaviour. These relationships were responsible for the wholeness of the system, which meant that whenever inflexible links changed irrespective of the reason, the behaviour of the system was destroyed. When inflexible links were destroyed, the system ceased to work. In a territorial production complex, for example, the role of these links was played by technological relations (extracting natural resources – stages of their processing – the production of finished goods – their consumption). Kolosovski's theory of energo-productive cycles was the first based on the concept of inflexible links. Into this category were numbered also the links taking the form of territorial networks of electric power, water supply and population provision with consumer goods (Kolosovski 1958).

The flexible links in territorial systems were those which could change when the system presented a particular state of its behaviour. The alteration of these links did not result in disturbing system's behaviour, that is, the system was able to adapt itself to the changes. The aim of flexible links was to help the existence of the internal organization of the territorial system, to balance the relationships amongst elements of the system and its relationship to the external environment. Flexible links included most of the relationships between production and the natural environment, between the population and the environment, the relationships among branches of the economy, transport links, and the relationships dealing with the servicing of the population (Blazhko 1976).

Relationships in territorial systems were also divided into material and immaterial. The former included, for example, streams of haulage, passengers, or energy, while the latter included, for example, flows of information and ideas. The formation and development of territorial systems depended increasingly on the last type of links.

What distinguished territorial systems from other systems was territorial structure. This was a structural characteristic typical only of territorial systems. According to Soviet geographers, this constituted the subject matter of human geography. The most vital problem was that of the distribution of geographical objects from the point of view of their mutual interrelationships. Primary roles were attributed to the objects with productive potential. By applying a systems approach, their mutual spatial relationships were investigated, together with the functional links among them. This meant that the territorial organization of a system was examined which, in turn, made it possible to define the rationality of the distribution of the elements and their relationships from the point of view of the most effective utilization of resources and the optimization of territorial relations (Aganbegian *et al.* 1972).

In order to disclose the territorial structure of a system it was necessary to delimit within it its smaller territorial units. These units should represent their own, functional wholeness, that is, each territorial subsystem should be a relatively isolated system. An important feature of a territorial system was its hierarchical nature. The essence of this nature consisted in the spatial divisibility of the system. Apart from structural characteristics, territorial systems possessed functional characteristics. The system in work caused its transformation, and changed its structural characteristics.

The systems approach to the study of territorial pattern found its best expression in the investigations of territorial production complexes. With the beginning of the 1970s these complexes were even termed 'territorial production systems'. Perhaps the largest work on this topic was carried out at the Institute of Economics and Organization of Industrial Production, Siberian Branch of the Soviet Academy of Sciences (Bandman 1971). According to the scholars working there, the system view was the most suitable for studying territorial systems in terms of the problem of the location of combinations of interrelated productive activities. Such work had certain peculiarities and called for new approaches and research techniques. Their emergence was caused by a number of factors. First, the increase in specialization of productive activities resulted in an intensification of intra-sector and inter-sector linkages. This caused a sharp increase in the role of optimization of the location and of the relationships of the units as a factor in raising productive efficiency. Second, an increase in the concentration of production put in new claims not only on the quantity of resources used directly, but also on the qualitative characteristics of the environment. The natural factor did not by any means lose its significance. On the contrary, its importance with respect to solving the problems of the location of productive activities had become greater. Third, both specialization and concentration in production changed essentially the conditions of manpower supply. Demands for the quantity and quality of manpower were higher than ever before. As a result, the dependence for the efficiency of alternative production locations on the size, composition and mobility of manpower, and on the established and future settlement systems became tighter. Fourth, the specialization and concentration of industrial units not only intensified the co-operation and combining of productive activities within industry, the linkages of industry with natural and manpower resources, but they also amplified the relationships of industry with the whole economic and social environment: productive and social infrastructure, population and administration. This all caused the emergence of new forms of regional productive forces (Bandman *et al.* 1971).

The changes in the conditions for the formation and functioning of productive activities not only increased the number of factors, but also turned some of them from those which were taken into consideration in an indirect manner to those which were directly involved in the process of solving problems. This widened substantially the dimensions and complicated the structure of one of the most important types of industrial geographic problems, that of optimizing the location and migration of productive activities. However, structural complexity was caused by the increase in the number of factors taken into consideration as much as by the intricacy and diversity of the forms of their influence, that is, the existence of direct and indirect, direct and inverse relationships between the factors and production and amongst the factors as well.

Not only did environment, infrastructure and manpower affect the location of productive activities, but the development of productive activities affected the state of the natural environment, the formation of infrastructure and manpower. In addition, an increase in the number of infrastructural elements caused by the emergence of a new development of an existing productive activity called for an increase in the number of working people. This required the expansion of infrastructure and, as a result, the increased population numbers and infrastructure enhanced the load on the natural environment. Conservation measures in their turn called for more labour and the development of particular infrastructure elements, and so forth. Thus, each direct relationship gave rise to an inverse one.

Both direct and inverse relationships might be direct and indirect, that is, they occurred between a pair of the research subjects directly or by means of a third one indirectly. For example, the investments in social infrastructure contributed to an improvement of living conditions for the population. As a consequence, the extent of people's attachment to the area increased, together with the opportunities to control the migration of the population. As a result, production was able to reduce expenditure in attracting and training the labour force.

It was difficult to take account of particular interrelationships, because of the fact that their effect manifested itself usually with a certain lag both in space and time. Without a proper examination of the whole interaction of locational factors it was impossible to determine the geography of a given productive activity. The above relationships manifested themselves differently according to variations in scale and in different natural and socio-economic conditions. This predetermined not only the varied role of the above conditions, but also the differentiating level at which each of them was examined. Both the role and the level were determined in each given case depending on the study objective, the subject peculiarities, the time duration, the scale of the region under study and socio-economic conditions. The most geographical dimension characterized the problems of industrial location and migration within regions. At this level, regional factors and interrelationships needed complex geographical study.

All this meant that problems of industrial location were solved as a part of a more general task, that of optimizing the structure of the whole economy of an area, and primarily, territorial production systems. One of the principal research directions was the elaboration of the system of models for long-term territorial production planning. Questions were dealt with at various levels of the system with regard to both space and sectors. With that end in view a number of models were proposed to solve a series of practical tasks:

- Emphasis was placed on taking account of the inter-sector linkages. Instead of the locational tasks for the units of one industry, those for a complex of interrelated industries were solved.
- Account was taken of direct and inverse relationships between industrial branches and particular infrastructure elements.
- Account was taken of the direct and inverse relationships between the production sector and the rest of the economy of a region, the population and the environment.

This last model was realized within a framework which used the technique of economic-mathematical modelling for optimizing the process of forming regional territorial production systems.

Conclusions

At the beginning of the 1980s, a social crisis gradually swept over the countries of the East European subregion, later embracing the Soviet Union. Geographers were disappointed with the inability of positivist geography to deal with relevant social problems. This resulted in a turning to humanistic and radical approaches which found their expression in emerging social geography. The development of social geography in the region is discussed in the next chapter.

5

Recent developments: the emergence of social geography

There were two basic reasons for the rapid development of social studies within East European–Soviet human geography in the decade of the 1980s: first, a socio-economic crisis that swept over the region, and second, the influence of new ideas in western geography. Both caused geographers to shift their interest from mainly economically-oriented studies to those oriented primarily to humans and human affairs. Work within the field was carried out predominantly in two countries: Poland and the USSR. Each country's output is discussed here in turn.

Social geography in Poland: a humanistic approach

The humanistic approach emerged in contemporary social geography in Poland in the second half of the 1980s primarily as a reaction to the crisis that seized Polish society at the beginning of the decade. This chapter is concerned with the nature of humanistic geography in terms of the underlying theoretical assumptions and problems constituting its subject matter. Both are deeply rooted in the traditions of the Polish school of sociology, particularly in the work of F. Znaniecki who introduced the idea of space into the discipline as early as the 1930s. His theory constitutes a significant part of the humanistic paradigm in contemporary social geography in Poland. In order to make the discussion clear, the basic assumptions of this theory are presented first, before humanistic geography is outlined. The text below is thus divided into two parts. In the first part, a brief outline of Znaniecki's approach to the concept of space is presented. The second part discusses major ideas and research problems of contemporary humanist geography in Poland.

The roots of contemporary humanist geography in Poland

Znaniecki's theory was presented in two works (Znaniecki 1931; 1938). The first work comprised some preliminary ideas concerning humanistic space. As Znaniecki pointed out in the foreword to his book (Znaniecki 1931), his approach emerged as a reaction to Park's urban ecology. Unlike Park and his followers, who considered the urban area as an objective socio-spatial structure, Znaniecki interpreted the territory of the city as being a humanistic whole being formed in human experience and activity. People occupy urban space, 'but they are not only things, however, but active subjects being able to experience what is around them, and from this point of view they are not within the city but – if one may say – the city is in their sphere of common experience and activity, they create it as a complex structure' (Znaniecki 1931, ix–x).

People living in the city constituted what Znaniecki termed 'a territorial community'. According to him, this was not an accidental or loose collection of individuals, but a group of individuals constituting a complex and highly rationalized structure, characterized by common purposeful activity and shared goals being pursued. Within such a community 'there is an interest in public affairs and a strong feeling of spiritual ties among one another owing to which the city can exist as a human whole' (xi). Urban space with people living in it and constituting a territorial community existed as a construct in the human mind (moral consciousness, as Znaniecki called it). People had particular attitudes to this spatial human whole, and in order to describe these attitudes Znaniecki focused his attention on so-called 'constructive social forces'. He used this term to define all the aims and aspirations resulting from the sense of duty (responsibility) that members feel they owe to their territorial community. These forces were identified as qualities or values from which the community benefits. 'What qualities and values the community possesses', wrote Znaniecki, 'in the moral consciousness of its members, and in which way it would use them if the ideals of its leaders were shared by all the community members enrich their social substance (essence) and increase their spiritual power' (1931, 8). These constructive social forces Znaniecki identified by study-ing the relations between members of the community. In addition, he went on to investigate the following: (1) the community understood as a system of institutions; (2) officials affiliated to the institutions, and (3) other members of the community.

Znaniecki presented his humanistic theory of space in a fuller version several years later (Znaniecki 1938). He made a distinction between geo-graphical and humanistic space. They were the only ones existing in the practice of social sciences. The first was absolute, featureless, objectively measurable, limitless and infinitely divisible. People and patterns of material things were distributed within it and processes occurred to change existing spatial structures. From the humanistic point of view, on the other hand, there was no such thing as an absolute space. 'Space for a humanist is one of many categories which he uses studying man. It is analogous to a myth, a language, a ceremony, a picture, and a researcher must take it with its human aspect, that is, in the way in which it is experienced by the human subjects he investigates' (90). According to Znaniecki, human experience was not provided by any universal, objective, featureless space within which other people and things move, including the subject experiencing this space. 'People give to their experiences innumerable spaces, qualitatively differentiated, limited and confirmed, indivisible, unstable and positively or negatively appreciated at the same time. The term "space" humanists should use generically, denoting the whole class of these specific and particular spaces' (91). Znaniecki proposed to speak rather about spatial values. None of the latter are independent: 'each is a component of a certain aspatial system of values, with reference to which such a spatial value acquires a specific meaning and essence. There are a variety of value systems, for example, religious, aesthetic, technical and productive, economic, social, etc.' (91).

According to Znaniecki, spatial value acquired a specific meaning with respect to the experience and activity of a social group. Such groups

possess in the sphere of their collective experience and activity certain spatial values which are treated as a common property of their own, not in a pure economic sense, but in a more general meaning, according to which groups rule these spatial values using them to accomplish certain collective activities [. . .]. Thus, for example, for a social group on a national scale such a spatial value is the territory of the country occupied by members of the group [. . .], for a religious group common spatial values, which are especially claimed to be ruled, are holy (sacred) places, although its property in its eyes is also the entire territory inhabited by coreligionists [. . .], for a productive group, the area under farm or factory, for a family its flat, for an association the place of its meetings – all these are social values considered as integral components of social group life.(92)

With the idea of group spatial value another concept was closely connected. This was the concept of ecological position. According to Znaniecki, the group, as a ruler of its spatial property (value), was entitled to permit individuals to occupy places within space. Such a right an individual was granted (bestowed) by the group. The spatial position which was acknowledged (admitted) to the individual depended, however, on his or her social role, or on where he or she stood in society. It was this position that Znaniecki termed the ecological one. Ecological position was thus the right to occupy a place within a common spatial property acknowledged to individuals by a group, which corresponded with their social position, and constituted a part of their social status (Znaniecki 1938).

These basic concepts of Znaniecki's theory of human ecology which have an explicit spatial connotation – the idea of urban space and territorial community on the one hand, and spatial value, group spatial value and ecological position on the other hand – have been adopted and developed recently by social geographers as a significant part of the theoretical assumptions that underpin humanistic studies in social geography in Poland.

Basic research fields and ideas of humanistic geography in Poland

As stated above, the major reason for the emergence of humanistic studies in Polish social geography has been the impact of the crisis that seized Polish society at the beginning of the 1980s. There has been some influence of western social geography; its role has proved inconspicuous, however, and it is mentioned only briefly.

Like every other sphere of life in Poland, the process of overwhelming crisis has affected social geography. Geographers have realized that neither the phenomena they study, nor the methods they applied and goals they pursued fit actual social problems or the ways these problems appear in their spatial setting. It has become obvious, not only for geographers, that social problems being manifested so severely should no longer be investigated and solved within the frameworks of separate social disciplines. The only reasonable action is to link the efforts of the social scientists in a common attempt to find a new, more realistic approach which will reinforce the capabilities of their disciplines to be more useful in solving practical problems of social reality.

The idea of initiating common investigations into spatial aspects of social phenomena was offered first of all by social geographers. Kuklinski (1984), arguing for focusing attention on relevant social problems in their spatial context, pointed out that there was still at least one potential existing within Polish society capable not merely of overcoming the present crisis, but also of ensuring continuous social development in the long term. This potential was the existence of local communities with well-developed systems of self-government. These communities, according to Kuklinski, should constitute the subject matter of socio-geographical studies. The goal of such studies was formulated more than fifty years ago by Znaniecki (1931), and it is worth quoting again: 'What are the constructive social forces of its members (resulting from the feeling of duty) that a local community really uses, and what are the ones it could use without prejudice to other social groups, if the ideal of its leaders being shared by all members of the community is to enrich its social essence (substance) and to increase its spiritual power?' (Znaniecki 1931, viii.)

A number of specialists representing various social disciplines contributed to the project. It is under their influence, notably that of sociologists and ethnologists, that the concepts and ideas of the Polish school of humanistic sociology, particularly those of Znaniecki, Ossowski and their followers, have been introduced and applied within the study on local communities, enriching the methodology and practice of socio-geographical enquiries. Two major problems have been proposed to structure investigations into these phenomena. On the one hand there has been the problem of how the local community (territorial group) is reflected in the consciousness of its members – what are their attitudes and related behaviour resulting from such conscious experience. On the other hand, the problem has dealt with the nature of local community, with the reasons, forces or factors that bind or link individuals together in groups, and the role played by the emotional attitudes that are given expression in the need to identify with the territorial group.

With regard to each of the two above problems, a different approach has developed; both are discussed below. First, investigations are presented concerning the local community as the phenomenon consciously experienced by its members; secondly, characteristics of local groups are outlined in terms of the bonds grouping people together to form small-scale territorial societies.

Local communities in the consciousness of their members

The first area of study on local communities involves attitudes and behaviour with respect to the consciously-experienced social environment. For human individuals, the local community is a social environment (context) in which a number of processes occur which are important for their lives. This is the fundamental process of socialization of individuals, creating their personalities and forming their opinions and outlook upon life. Within the conditions that the local community provides, moral values and social norms are reproduced, criteria are created for the evaluation and appreciation of various attitudes, aspirations and motives. At the same time, the value system arises and is shaped, enabling individuals to understand their role in community life and to work out their attitudes towards facts, events and processes occurring within the changing world around them (Dyoniziak 1978).

Through these processes, individuals (and their groups) not only adapt to the social environment but are also able to influence it actively, bringing about changes in its structure. It is often assumed for an ideal situation that the structure of the local community is susceptible to changes, constituting the context within which individuals can act as human agents according to the rights which are vested in them (Johnston 1986). The question, however, arises whether such an assumption is valid in every socio-political circumstance, especially in those which not so very recently were typical of Poland (and to which the studies presented here refer). Investigations on local groups has taken this question into account, focusing attention on the constraints of various natures imposed on human agency by social structure in the context characteristic of a local community. The relationship between structure and human agency is interpreted here in a way typical of the humanistic approach. According to it, the structure is investigated in terms of a certain image appearing in human consciousness, whereas human agency is viewed in terms of opinions, attitudes and behaviour revealed by individuals (and their groups) under the influence of this image.

The study of local communities can be divided into two distinct classes. In the first class, investigations concern the major components of which the structure of social life within the territorial community is composed. These investigations can be called 'monographic' studies. The second class involves particular phenomena entering into the composition of the life-world of the territorial group.

MONOGRAPHIC STUDIES

There are various combinations of phenomena examined in this class of study, and their selection depends primarily on the goal of the investigation. In one such study the aim was to recognize whether there were differences, and if so, how large they were, in opinions and attitudes towards certain aspects of local reality (or spheres of social life) as seen by people living in three local communities different in size and character, or in other words, to recognize how the circumstances of distinct social environments shaped human agency (or attitudes to the territorial group). Certain phenomena were distinguished as those which most differentiated people's attitudes, namely: the level of material well-being, economic contradictions, conflicts in the place of work, earning levels, participation in the illegal economy, social disparities and local power (Boczkowski et al. 1988; Hryniewicz 1989).

In another investigation, the social life of a territorial group was analysed in terms of the conflict between structure and human agency. This problem was described and accounted for using the concept of the social formation of space. In this study, the process was analysed whereby social relations are shaped under the influence (impact) of the institutions and organizations located within the territory of local community. These subordinate, tame and mark the space, transforming it into the place of social life (Blasiak et al. 1988). Not every activity, however, converts space into a place suitable for human needs. What distinguishes such a place are social relationships going beyond the range of narrow family ties, indispensable enough to convert a social group occupying the place into a local community. Otherwise, a group constitutes what one may term a 'local mass', where family relations take precedence over those having a wider social range. What serves to transform a local mass into a local community is a specific form of activity directed to the local needs of a social group. This activity can be termed a local one. On the other hand, an activity which is not local in character is incapable of creating a local community, and induces processes which disintegrate social relations, converting a social group into a local mass. A large part of the activities of a centrally-planned economy are of the latter character. They were situated in the structure of local communities as elements not conducive to the formation of territorial societies, and responsible for the process of their destruction.

Conflict between structure and human agency as consciously experienced by human individuals has also been investigated from the point of view of how far it was advanced, and whether there were self-defence mechanisms mobilizing people against the activity of organizations to oppose the process of community destruction (Blasiak et al. 1988). A similar study was carried out by Szczepanski (1989) who also investigated an urban territorial community. He combined two points of view: that referring to the phenomenon of everyday life, and that concerning the process of the social formation of space. The point was to study how the socially created space influenced the process of consolidation or disintegration of the local community and how this was manifested through the activities constituting the everyday life of human individuals.

Much work on local community structures has been based on the model proposed by Znaniecki (1931). The institutions of the local community, their officials, and various social groups, classes, strata and associations are investigated in terms of how they are mentally experienced, and then attitudes towards these components of local life are analysed to account for different forms of human agency (Beba and Murawska 1985; Hryniewicz 1988; Piotrowski et al. 1988).

STUDIES CONCERNING PARTICULAR ASPECTS OF THE SOCIAL LIFE OF THE TERRITORIAL GROUP

The second type of study of local communities as they appear in the human mind concern particular phenomena characteristic of the structure of social life within the community. Three phenomena have attracted the particular attention of researchers: (1) the structure and elites of local power; (2) the local press, and (3) collective activities.

Local power elites can be studied from the point of view of not only the members of the territorial group, but also of their officials and servants. Investigations have concerned the problem of participation in the structures of local power (who, and using which criteria); relations, both personal and institutional, within these structures (Glowacki 1988); the problem of alienation of local power (Boczkowski *et al.* 1988); stereotypes of civil servants in terms of their competences, qualifications and the confidence they enjoy; stereotypes of institutions in terms of their reputation, usefulness and the forms of constraints they impose on the social life of a territorial group (Gumula 1988; Gieorgica and Dutkiewicz 1986; Bugalski 1988). Some investigations have approached the problem of local power in terms of changes over time, taking into account the role of cultural traditions and historic heritage in analysing how people experience the institutions ruling local life (Halamska 1989).

The local press constitutes an important factor in the process of socialization of members of a territorial group. Oniszczuk (1989) specifies the role which the local press plays in the everyday life of people. Two basic systems of local information were shown to exist: an official (formal) system, and an informal one consisting primarily of interpersonal contacts. People used the first to receive information from formal sources, and the other to spread, to complete and to interpret this information. The latter helped form opinions and attitudes constituting a counterweight to the formal information which was devoid of social feelings. In effect, the so-called model of participating social communication took the place of the one-sided model of official information. The former created circumstances to develop the individual's subjectivity as a specific form of human agency within constraints produced by the social structure of the local community (Oniszczuk 1982; Mikulowski-Pomorski 1988).

Another specific form of human agency appearing in the territorial group is the phenomenon of collective activity – action undertaken by groups of people to meet their needs and aspirations and to benefit the local community as a whole (Turska 1988). Znaniecki treated this form of local activity as a very important element in his concept of constructive social forces, interpreting it as a significant factor in local group development (Znaniecki 1931). Investigations of collective activity have concerned the problem of how such activity was seen by members of the territorial group, and their attitudes to that form of participation in the life of the local community. Those attitudes were analysed in terms of the differences between actual forms of performing collective activities, and the so-called obligatory model or norm relating to these activities, existing in human consciousness and having its origins in cultural traditions and values (Turska 1989).

The nature of local community – the problems of bonds grouping people together

The point of view proposed so far has stressed primarily one major aspect of the nature of local community, according to which it is a fragment of a larger social structure, possessing a number of significant features of the latter, and as such, constituting the context of everyday lives. There is another aspect, however, of the nature of local community. This is the social context, or social environment, which the local community forms (creates) for its members, and which constitutes a certain place in space with which people are linked in a wide variety of ways.

Unlike the concept of a local community where the environment was mainly of a functional character consisting of organizations, institutions and different social groups, the environment considered in this approach is not only functional, but also has a marked cultural element. It constitutes what is often termed a human place, which has emerged in the long history of the relationship between people and the natural environment, in the course of which the latter has been marked, tamed and adapted to human needs (Jalowiecki 1986). Such a place is close to people in an emotional sense. They are linked and attached to it by values and symbols related to local tradition and myth, confirming people's identity with a territorial group and distinguishing it from other territorial groups (Dobrowolska 1985). This is the form in which the phenomenon of a sense of place is given its expression. Through it such aspects of the affective ties with place are revealed as the sense of belonging, of intimacy, of security, of being at home and of having control over place.

The above point of view, concerning the attitude towards territorial group in the form of identity and attachment or simply of the sense of place, makes it easier to examine the problem of the nature of local community (territorial group). As indicated earlier, this nature is primarily determined by the form and character of links within the local community. Considerations of this problem came from original attempts to define the territorial range of local communities. The difficulties often met in doing that posed the question of what the local community represented. Did this peculiar form of social life still exist within contemporary society characterized by increasing anonymity of members, formalization and objectivization of human relations, disintegration of social ties, disorganization of human life within the course of contemporary processes of institutionalization and segmentation of society? (Wierzbicki 1987). For a long time, there has been a conviction among social scientists that the above processes would lead to the disappearance of local communities. Investigations conducted in Poland during the 1970s, and particularly the 1980s suggested that this was not the case. Local communities still exist but they operate at a different level of social activity and have different forms. Their most characteristic attribute is that they are in a continuous process of change, affected by outside processes which imply transforming and modifying the structure of territorial groups to adapt to the changing world around them (Sliwinska 1989; Sadowski 1989).

Among the bonds grouping people in territorial communities, Wieruszewska (1989) distinguishes two kinds: functional bonds, referring to people, functions, actions and relations among them, and what she calls cultural bonds, arising from the sense of unity of values related to the local community as a certain common whole which has a specific, symbolic meaning for its members. The former are related to local functions provided by a territorial community and, besides economic, political and organizational ones, include those constituting the spheres of socialization, social control, participation, mutual aid and so on; the latter concern social relations which are rooted in the cultural sphere, in the sphere of common values (Wieruszewska 1989). This division reflects the state of studies on the nature of local community. This is analysed within two separate research fields, each of which is discussed below.

STUDIES OF FUNCTIONAL BONDS WITHIN THE TERRITORIAL COMMUNITY

Research on bonds taking the form of social functions and relations are relatively rare, and few works have appeared. There is only one which concerns the adaptation of the local community to changes occurring in the world outside (Sadowski 1989). The author's focus is on rural communities. According to him they

have not only disappeared but still exist retaining a relatively high degree of autonomy, and they are often places where traditional values are revived, presenting new modern and functional forms in an industrialized society (. . .). Thus, the closed local communities existing formerly have passed on the values characteristic of broader social structures and developed new relations and links which enable them to integrate in a new, both organizational and spatial form.(3.)

Another example is a study concerning which of the three major elements constituting territorial community (that is, a culturally transformed territory (place), the social group occupying it, or symbolic determinants of the social and spatial identity of territorial groups) is most significant for the process of forming and maintaining a territorial group, and it is suggested that such an element is that of social interaction among members of a social community (Dobrowolska 1985). There are also a few works within this research field that deal with the nature of urban communities. Attempts have been made to recognize these communities in the complex structures of urban social space, and to identify ties which link people together to form territorial groups (Sliwinska 1989; Wodz 1989).

What is characteristic of the above studies is that local community appears as a specific common whole in the eyes of its members. This is similar to the second research field outlined below in which the focus is not so much on the bonds that are 'horizontal', occurring among people, as on the ties of a 'vertical' nature, related to the place.

STUDIES OF EMOTIONAL AND CULTURAL BONDS WITHIN THE TERRITORIAL COMMUNITY

'Vertical' links are of an emotional character, taking the form of attitudes that reveal a feeling of identity with place and an attachment to the territorial group. This kind of bond implies some consideration of the nature of local community in terms of cultural categories and phenomena.

For emotional bonds to form, a system of common values must be accepted by members of a territorial community, or in other words, a sphere is required constituting the cultural system of the local group (Wieruszewska 1989). The sense of common ties rests on 'tradition, continuity, persistence, common memory, coherence of internal relations centring around certain leading values' – categories that together define a certain system of symbols that people use to identify with a particular area and the social group occupying it. It is this 'internally experienced attachment contained in a symbolic sphere that constitutes the interpretation of the sense the members of a territorial group attribute to their community' (Wieruszewska 1989, 5).

Among the categories enabling people to recognize their group as a common symbol, a particular role is played by a spatial value, or a 'group spatial value' as first defined by Znaniecki. It takes the form of collective (group) images of a place considered by people as their own, as a group value or its property. Members of the social group perceive and experience particular elements of their place, and treat them as their own from the point of view of symbolic meanings these elements present to the group. Such a common spatial value is as a rule strictly related to the history of the community and is conveyanced only to its members. Meanings related to this value, to symbolic elements distinguished in the territory (place) occupied by social group, are transformed into a common cultural characteristic of its members, constituting at the same time the elements enhancing the feeling of attachment (Wodz 1989).

Wallis (1979) points out the significance of this common, cultural spatial value calling it a 'cultural area'. It is specified by images, representations and symbols related to temples, cemetaries, monuments, urban quarters and places of antiquity related to the history of the community. All these symbolic spaces constitute a permanent memory of this community. 'Pointing out such an area, we confirm thereby the existence of the group or community which uses it, is linked with it in a variety of ways, and identifies with it' (Wallis 1979, 70).

Spatial value, or the cultural area, has an internal character related to a particular territorial group to be recognized first of all by its members. Ossowski (1960) claimed that, besides internal values, there were also values of an external character whose importance for group cohesion was no less significant. Those values created what he called 'convincing bonds'. He distinguished between two aspects of the connection between an individual and a territorial group. The first was reflected in the notion of 'private homeland', the other in the term 'ideological homeland'. The former was related to the world of the everyday life of individuals, while the latter was related to the global community which is the nation. 'The meanings people give to the concept of private homeland reflect personal attitudes to their life-worlds. They value things constituting these worlds, call them their own, and thereby these things become extensions of their personalities' (210). The attitude towards ideological homeland, on the other hand, is expressed by an individual's participation in national community. 'These attitudes rest neither on immediate experiences with respect to native territory nor on customs and habits created by these experiences, but on a conviction: on the conviction that they participate in a certain community as a one common whole, and on the conviction that it is this community (whole) that is related just to this territory' (210).

In its internal aspect community exists by its views in the consciousness of its members. These views are, however, binding by external values attributed to the group as a whole [. . .] These values generate a significant link among individuals. Such a link is based on individuals' convictions that all the members of the group share these values in the same way, which creates certain common desires and emotional attitudes, as well as the forms of the community life which depend on these values' (216–217).

It is this shared conviction that gives the territorial group the meanings of symbols, senses or values, and a specific image of the territorial group as something unique and exceptional.

Studies of the nature of local community in terms of the attitudes of an emotional character, or of the sense of place, concern territorial groups of various sizes related to villages, towns, urban quarters and areas on a subregional scale occupied by ethnic groups. Early work on the problem of identification with the territorial group was undertaken with regard to urban communities, primarily those related to housing estates within large cities (Jalowiecki 1980; Jalowiecki and Nurek 1980; Jalowiecki 1982; Nurek 1982). The investigations used the assumptions of a semiotic approach, according to which territory appeared in human consciousness as a set of signs: 'space, as an objectivized man-made entity, can be defined besides its pure material aspect using other names: a cultural universe, symbolic system or outlook upon life – this is so, it is an ordered sequence of territorially inscribed signs to be communicated to a receiver' (Nurek 1982, 24). Such a point of view analysed the meanings which the territory imparted to people. The study of the semiotic structure (the meaning of space) of housing estates consisted in specifying the meanings that people allocated to various fragments of the environment within which they lived. The meanings constituted particular images in their consciousness which underpinned their attitudes towards that environment.

The same problem of identity with the place which was the housing estate was interpreted in terms of Znaniecki's concept of ecological position (Bialas 1982). Such a place occupied by a social group was transformed into a common collective value integrating members of the community. According to the right that the community possessed as a ruler of spatial value, it specified the ecological position of members by regulating their presences and places within the space according to their social roles. These roles were interpreted in terms of the tendency to occupy the most favourable position in space. Bialas proved that there was stability in the way the roles (ecological positions) were performed. Social space (environment) 'exerts an influence on human behaviour that causes socio-spatial situations to form a sequence (pattern) corresponding with social roles, structures, life cycles in order to assist and enhance these relations of which this environment is the result' (Bialas 1982, 308). In his investigations of social links grouping people into territorial communities, Bialas confirmed Ossowski's idea of the convinced bond. The housing estate (community) appeared in the consciousness of inhabitants not only in terms of local categories, but in terms of those characteristics of global urban life. 'The way people define situations which mould their behaviour as inhabitants, is based rather on the knowledge of the positive and negative sides of urban life, on global values rather than on local ones' (304).

In another study (Mikulowski-Pomorski 1986), the same phenomenon of attachment to a territorial group occupying a housing estate was analysed using Znaniecki's concept of ecological position. This concept was employed in a broader context, however. The ecological position of a territorial group was studied within the space which was the property of the city represented by the city authorities that were rulers of urban spatial value. The investigations aimed to define the relationship between the ecological position of a housing estate community (the possibility of ruling the place it occupied) and the degree of identification of its members towards their place of living.

The central problem of Znaniecki's theory concerning social wholes (groups) as they are experienced by their members has also been explored in rural communities. Wieruszewska (1987), using data for four rural communities in different parts of Poland, investigated them from the point of view of the possibilities for creating an environment capable of inducing feelings of identification and attachment. The purpose was to analyse

the extent to which the contemporary villages situated in different parts of the country, presenting certain social and cultural wholes (at least in terms of remembered or culti- vated traditions, customs, habits, norms and functions which have the aim of maintaining the system, that is to say, functions of an educational, controlling and protecting character) can still be those environs that influence the identification and specify the identity of their inhabitants. (Wieruszewska 1987, 173.)

Perhaps the most typical and clear form of territorial community is that of the ethnic group. In contemporary Poland these groups are under the influence of two opposing tendencies. On the one hand there is the tend- ency to disintegration, the main reason for which has been a long-lasting mutual relationship with the ethnic majority which is the Polish nation. On the other hand, a contrary trend has emerged recently, consisting in a sudden revival of ethnic self-consciousness and self-interest directed towards the values and symbols relating to many aspects of social life. The latter tendency is strictly related to deep social changes occurring in Poland, and to a large degree is a direct consequence of them. This finds its expression mainly in cultural phenomena or movements. It is now the subject of a number of studies that concern those aspects of culture and social life through which the phenomena of integration are particularly clearly articulated. The investigations are intended to define how identifica- tion and attachment are reflected in a variety of forms which assume cul- tural aspects of integration within ethnic minorities in Poland (Synak 1988; Iskierski 1989; Jedruch 1988; Zeranska-Kominek 1989).

Within the humanistic model presented here, there is some research concerning the problem of the world created in human consciousness which is not necessarily related to the phenomenon of the territorial group. This work originated mainly under the influence of the humanistic approach developed in western social geography. In Polish socio-geographical studies this approach has focused mainly on the problem of the sense of place.

Sense of place has been explored in various ways. Rykiel (1984) analysed it in terms of how various spatial structures of a cultural character were reflected in language, mainly in colloquial speech. Libura (1988) examined the attitudes towards a particular place, interviewing people from different parts of Poland. The sense of place was analysed by Sieminski (1989), using examples of its images presented in literature. Zaleska (1989) investigated the sense of place in terms of sentiments people associated with different fragments of urban space, mainly of a historic character, and Bartkowski (1988) attempted to identify what feelings are related to the centre of the city, as a symbol of identification with place.

Conclusions

The essential problems related to the nature of contemporary humanistic geography in Poland have been presented above. Studies within the field have developed relatively quickly, mostly as a response to the crisis which has so severely affected Polish society. The studies have been applied primarily to the one problem, the examination of which is considered critical for the development of knowledge and understanding of these crisis phenomena in space. This is the problem of local communities (territorial groups) which has been investigated by social geographers from two points of view. On the one hand, there is the question of how the local community is reflected in the consciousness of its members and what constitutes their attitudes and related human behaviour resulting from such experience. On the other hand, there is the issue of the nature of the local community, the reasons that bind individuals together in the group, and the role played by the emotional attitudes that are given expression in the need to identify with the territorial group and to feel attached to it. The main trends which have developed in humanistic geography in Poland in connection with studying the phenomenon of territorial community have been reviewed here. They have been discussed in terms of basic research problems as well as ideas and concepts applied to explain these problems.

Contemporary developments in social geography in the former Soviet Union

In this section the content of contemporary Soviet social geography is presented in terms of its subject matter and underlying theoretical assumptions. The focus is on the major approaches applied currently in the discipline. After a summary of the historical reasons which have led to the present situation in the field, there is an analysis of the main areas of research that have developed within the discipline.

Introduction

The first study dealing with social problems in space was carried out in 1877 by P. P. Semenov-Tyan-Shanski, and Regent (1980) considers this the beginning of social geography in Russia. This was an analysis of a few communities of the Muraevo locality near Moscow, from the point of view of the changes in the social and economic status of population created by the enfranchisement reform of 1861. Semenov-Tyan-Shanski identified social stratification and spatial variation in wealth and described them in terms of different classes of households which he distinguished on the basis of land property and income (Regent 1980). Later, social geography studies were undertaken within anthropogeography which developed in the last decades of the nineteenth century and lasted to the end of the 1920s (Hooson 1968).

The form and character of contemporary social geography in the former USSR is influenced primarily by events and changes that occurred in geography during the emergence and first decades of the existence of the Soviet state. The new political, economic and social order created then required new solutions consistent with the goals to be pursued. One of the most important was to reconstruct the national economy. It was assumed that the only way to accomplish this was through economic growth. Lenin, who headed work on reconstruction, understood this growth not only as operating over time, but also as having a spatial dimension, finding its expression in the phenomenon of the territorial division of labour. It was he, perhaps, who first investigated this phenomenon using the concept of an economic region, and who included methods of regionalization in planning the reconstruction of the national economy (Saushkin 1966). Appreciating the role of the geographical factor in studying the problems of economic development, and facing at the same time the lack of specialists in spatial problems and issues, Lenin in 1921 created a new discipline which he called 'economic geography' (its aim was to study territorial aspects of economic processes using methods of regionalization). This was introduced as a new subject in university studies (Mereste and Nommik 1984).

That decision had a crucial impact on the future development of social geography in the Soviet Union. As stated above, this geography had developed earlier in the form of anthropogeographical studies. The new decision changed that situation radically. Anthropogeographical studies were banned, and for the following fifty years or so human geography was dominated by economic geography. Attempts to form other branches of geographical enquiry concerning different forms of human activity were thwarted. The concepts of economic region, economic regionalization, territorial productive forces and energo-productive cycles were the only significant ones to be explored, and even later, when other disciplines emerged, the influence of the economic tradition was so strong that analogies to these economic categories were sought for the phenomena constituting the subjects of the new research fields (Saushkin 1977; Mironenko 1988).

Two exceptions to this emerged, however. Both considered people with reference to their environments and both used the term 'social geography'. The first to use this term was N.N. Baranskiy in 1930. He investigated such phenomena as: the quality of people; the quality of their lives; their culture, likes and dislikes; their habits, political attitudes and social order. He pointed out the benefit gained from exploring social groups, and from providing insight into their nature, psychology and spirit as well as spatial differentiation of such phenomena (Baranskiy 1980).

Baranskiy's student, P. M. Kabo, proposed the concept of socio-cultural geography (Kabo 1947). His work was an original attempt to combine two kinds of factors conditioning the relations between people and their environment. He distinguished first general factors, operating beyond the control of individuals. What constituted such factors were social relations and the productive forces of the society, the latter made up of social groups occupying certain environments. Second, there were local factors, the character of which were closely related to specific circumstances of this environment and to the nature of human individuals forming territorial groups. The essence of the relationship between humans and the environment was defined by social relations and the level of development of productive forces. The peculiarity of this relationship, on the other hand, its local colour, depended on human activity determined to a large degree by environmental circumstances. The environment, being transformed in the course of human action, reflected characteristic cultural features of the social group occupying it. At the same time, however, it affected human life, marking it with attributes which constituted what Kabo termed the way of life. This concept involved all aspects of human life and activity in a particular environment. It was shaped both by human consciousness and by the peculiarities of the environment and the social organization of production. The way of life and characteristics of various areas formed the phenomena of territorial groups of people which entered into mutual relationships with one another, creating larger patterns which Kabo called socio-cultural territorial systems. Those systems, and territorial groups as their subsystems, were the subject matter of socio-cultural geography. According to Kabo, this was the discipline which studied how the ways of life of people were environmentally conditioned, what spatial patterns they presented, and those complex combinations of elements of which every socio-territorial group of people was composed (Kabo 1947).

Neither Baranskiy's nor Kabo's attempts to introduce human beings into the scope of economic geography met with much support and were neglected for many years until social geography re-emerged. Contemporary social geography emerged in the Soviet Union in the late 1960s, when population geography separated from economic geography, and the first signs of a deeper interest in people as the subject of the studies re-appeared (Kovalev 1966; Kovalev and Pokshishevskiy 1967; Alekseyev 1984; Mironenko 1988). The term 'social geography' started to be used in the early 1970s, and the word 'social' first appeared officially in 1978 when the Department of Higher Education ratified the subject called 'socio-economic geography' (Agafonov 1984).

The slow process of the creation of social geography was part of a wider process characteristic of Soviet human geography in the late 1960s. This consisted of two opposite tendencies. On the one hand, there was the disintegration of economic geography, its 'sociologization' (Tkachenko 1982), manifested in new research fields concerning the problems studied from a social rather than an economic perspective. On the other hand, there has been a contrary trend to prolong the dominant position of economic geography within human geography, a way of thinking that has a forty-year-old tradition (Mironenko 1988). This contradiction finds its expression in the question of the definition of social geography, its nature, subject matter and the place it occupies within human geography. There have been two opposite points of view concerning this problem (Raitviir 1984). According to the first one, social geography is an independent discipline which, together with economic geography, enters into the composition of human geography (Gochman 1979; Nommik 1979, 1982; Vabar 1981; Anokhin and Fedorov 1985) – the system of subjects that developed on the border between geography and social sciences, social geography embracing those subdisciplines which developed mainly on the border with sociology. The second point of view assumes that social geography is not an independent research field. It is either a subdiscipline of population geography, dealing with the spatial organization of social life within territorial systems of socio-economic activity (Dolinin 1976; Anokhin and Kostaev 1980; Lappo 1981), or it is simply a social aspect of economic geography. The subject matter is thus economic in its nature, and social aspects are distinguished in order better to grasp the many-sided nature of reality (Saushkin 1980; Lavrov and Sdasyuk 1980; Alayev 1982; Tkachenko 1982).

At present, the first approach is more widespread in Soviet literature. According to it, there are three main disciplines constituting the research field of human geography (*obshchestvennaya geografia*): social geography, economic geography and the discipline that emerged on the border of the two, namely socio-economic geography (Nommik 1979, 1982). The latter is not simply the sum of the other two, but their generalized synthesis and conceptual superstructure. Socio-economic geography involves only those aspects of the other two which allow achieving a better understanding of the dialectical unity of the world of social and economic appearances. The subject matter of socio-economic geography are socio-economic spatial complexes (systems) within which the cycle of social reproduction is completed (Tkachenko 1982; Alayev 1983; Palamarchuk 1983; Sharigin 1984; Lavrov, Anokhin and Agafonov 1984). The task of socio-economic geography is 'to study the regularities of territorial patterns of consumption of goods and services socially produced for the needs of the material and spiritual development of people, as well as geographical differences emerging in the various ways of life of people' (Nommik 1979, 4).

In practice, there is little connection between social and economic geography via the wide and somewhat abstract concept of socio-economic geography. Social geographers are more attracted by the ideas of other social sciences, as well as by those developed earlier in Russian geography. According to Alekseyev and Kovalev (1987), there are two broad classes of phenomena constituting the subject matter of contemporary social geography in the Soviet Union. These are, on the one hand, the problem of way of life, and on the other hand, the phenomenon of the local community, or territorial group of people. Studies concerning the two topics are discussed below.

Studies of way of life

The aim of investigations into the phenomenon of way of life is to grasp the essence of the interdependence between people and their environment. Such studies involve every kind of human activity taking place in the environment that tends to convert and adapt the environment as a place for human habitation. Focusing attention on all human activities makes it difficult to define the concept of way of life. Raitviir (1979) describes it as 'a characteristic of particular groups of people, a prevalent way of satisfying their needs and requirements within the course of everyday life and activity in given natural and socio-economic conditions' (46).

A variety of phenomena and processes are concealed by this definition, embracing all possible spheres of human everyday life from work to entertainment. The character of human activity and life varies and acquires different meanings according to the circumstances of natural and social environments, their structure, and the factors over which individuals and groups have little or no control: political, economic and cultural ones, as well as the attitudes and intentions of other people, their attributes, their likes, dislikes and customs revealed at the level of behaviour of individuals. All this creates a complex subject matter which social geographers attempt to set in order.

Alekseyev (1983, 1984) and Raitviir (1984) are of the opinion that there are four major components entering into the composition of the phenomenon of way of life, namely: the subject of the phenomenon; life conditions; human activities, and human consciousness. The subject is either a social group, or the human individual as a member of such a group. The concept of the group has various meanings; most often, however, it is specified with regard to either the size of area, or a group structure. The size of area a group occupies ranges from small units such as family or neighbourhood to larger ones such as regions or even the nation. The problem of group structure is simplified to some extent since Soviet society is by definition classless, and the basis for the distinctions are as a rule professional, socio-economic or national status (Lauristin, Kruusvall and Raitviir 1975; Raitviir 1979; Rivkina 1979, 1985; Khachatryants 1981; 'The ways of improvements of a socialist way of life 1982'). Life conditions involve the influence of the natural environment, the character and quality of the social infrastructure, work conditions, quality of life, the level of cultural development, the state and nature of political and social relations (Alekseyev 1984). As to activity, various forms of human everyday life are considered such as work and various forms of professional interest, home and household activities, leisure and social engagements (Raitviir 1979; Rivkina 1979; Alekseyev 1984). The description of way of life is not complete unless human consciousness is considered. Life conditions and everyday activities find their expression in human awareness. Living conditions are perceived, estimated and valued; the activity is analysed and compared with respect to needs and expectations, and to the system of values, norms and motives. Hence, the attitude of the human individual towards the surrounding world and other people is formed and shaped, and this governs behaviour, conduct and activity (Alekseyev 1984; Alekseyev and Kovelev 1987).

In practice, all four components (aspects) are rarely considered together since problems with data collection and handling increase very quickly. More often, some of the components are selected and their combinations investigated as an approximation of the phenomena of the way of life. Usually the components are coupled into pairs where one element, namely the subject, remains always the same. The pairs thus differ with regard to the other component. Raitviir (1984) distinguishes four such combinations (the other component is mentioned only): (1) living conditions; (2) human activity; (3) human consciousness, and (4) living conditions, activity and consciousness together, often termed the way of life in a broad sense. The above aspects or components, each one combined with the subject, define four major research areas within which investigations of way of life have been conducted. They are presented below.

Living conditions as way of life

The study of living conditions remains perhaps the most classical model of investigating the relationship between people and their environment. The focus is on how people live within a given environment (usually an urban one) which is generally defined in terms of social, economic and cultural categories. People that occupy urban territory differ in a number of attributes, but at the same time the territory presents a complex mosaic of characteristics. In Soviet cities, the most distinguishing attributes are socio-economic, material and ethnic status; age and family size; and, with respect to the territory, the distribution of service facilities, housing conditions and age of territorial units (Barbash and Raitviir 1986).

The differentiation of urban space is the result of a long-lasting process of city formation and development. In this process people play an important role when interacting with the environment; they transform it and give it a specific character. Within this mutual relationship between people and the environment, and as a result of differences among people in terms of their various styles of life, ways of satisfying needs, and modes of behaviour, as well as distinctions in the quality and character of the physical environment, a heterogeneous urban space is produced, presenting a mosaic of different ways of life which are manifested as various living conditions in various places. This is an objective process which occurs in cities within a centrally-planned economy. Urban social space remains heterogeneous because there are differences primarily of a demographic and cultural nature, and it is hardly likely that an optimal structure will arise for all social groups as various planning agencies intend, since 'what is good for one is now always so for others' (Barbash 1977).

In the USSR, investigations of way of life interpreted in terms of living conditions have mainly been factorial ecology studies. Various social phenomena have been investigated to present these conditions from a large variety of points of view. The phenomena investigated range from those of everyday activities to those related to various forms of social pathologies. The first such study was that of Barbash (1977) and concerned the Moscow conurbation. Moscow has been studied further (Barbash, Gimpelson and Davidovich 1985) along with other large cities in the Soviet Union, for example Tbilisi (Gheghechidze 1982), Kazan (Rukavishnikov 1980) and Tallin (Rukavishnikov 1980; Raitviir 1988).

Human activity as way of life

In the study of human activity, the focus is on different aspects of the phenomenon of way of life. People in relation to the environment is the central point of investigations, and more precisely, the complex mosaic of activities people carry out in their everyday lives. What is essential in such studies is to order the mosaics. This is done by distinguishing certain elementary forms of behaviour and activity, which when combined among one another in various ways allow the description of complex real world patterns. These elementary forms are termed stereotypes of human behaviour and activity (Alekseyev *et al.* 1975). They are characterized by two basic attributes: (1) a relative permanence in time, and (2) spatial distribution. Combining them, a wide variety of forms of human activity can be categorized into types or classes. Thus, in terms of the human activity approach, way of life is interpreted as the system of activity stereotypes within the everyday lives of people (Alekseyev *et al.* 1975).

According to the classification commonly used in these studies, way of life interpreted as the system of everyday human activities is divided into two broad categories: one related to the sphere of work and professional activity, the other to all the activities beyond the world of work. Within the latter there are further categories (classes) distinguished, such as: (1) satisfying subsistence and physiological needs; (2) home work; (3) leisure; (4) education and self-education, and (5) social activity. These classes are divided, in turn, into smaller categories to distinguish simpler forms of human activity and behaviour (Gordon and Klopov 1972; *Balans vremeni naselenia Latviyskoy SSR* 1976; Mints and Nepomnyatsiy 1979; Udaltsova 1981). The most common category used in investigations of human activities is that of the time budget. Everyday activities that individuals accomplish are recorded over a specified time, usually a day or a week, and way of life is presented in the form of the inputs spent on particular kinds of activity.

Studies of way of life using the concept of time budget concern populations which vary in size and structure. Some investigations deal with the entire country or a region (Dolenko and Savinov 1986) or a city (*Byudzhet vremeni gorodskogo naselenia* 1976). They may concern the whole population

(*Balans vremeni naselenia Latviyskoy SSR* 1976), the active population only (Karpukhin and Kuznetsova 1972; Klichyus 1974), or one occupational group. Such studies refer either to all types of activity (Mints and Niepomnyatsiy 1979) or are focused on one type, often leisure, presenting this in some detail (Gordon and Klopov 1972).

Human consciousness as an aspect of way of life

Studies of human consciousness concern people, both as individuals and as groups, in terms of their relationship to the environment, and the central problem is how this environment is perceived, appreciated and valued, and their attitudes to the surrounding world resulting from this mental experience. All this experience together constitutes a process, the output of which is human behaviour and activity which creates a significant fragment of the way of life. For the most part, studies deal with the urban environment, although works have recently appeared concerning the rural environment.

The environment is interpreted here as an object with regard to which people play the role of the subject (Mikhailov 1983; Stepanov 1983). The subject is considered either as a human individual or as a group. Stepanov (1989) suggests a third interpretation of 'man' as the subject. This is what he calls a social role. The social role, as the subject of the environment, is defined as a stereotype of consciousness and behaviour in which are reflected motives, expectations, deeds and feelings of either the group or particular individuals which are characteristic of the role that this individual or group performs in society.

There are two major assumptions made concerning the problem of how the environment is consciously experienced by the subject. First, the environment is part of a real, objective world, existing independently of the subject and not susceptible to distortion by subjective acts of perception. The subject can record the structure of the environment in his or her mind and evaluate its elements, endowing them with meanings. Such a point of view implies that there are two worlds existing separately from each other – the real one, and that imagined in the human mind. Second, it is assumed that there is only one world, combining the above two. The object (the environment) is not opposed to the subject, that is, it does not exist as any entity beyond the subject's consciousness. Environment interpreted as the outside world acts only in relation to its image. Attitude to the environment is reflexive in its character and consists in the emotional interpretation of all that surrounds people, in identifying with it, and in affecting and transforming it according to people's own motives, intentions, needs and beliefs (Savchenko 1983, Kostinskiy 1989).

With each of the above assumptions concerning the relationship between the environment and its image in human consciousness, a distinct class of phenomena is considered, forming the subject matter of different studies. Investigations concerning the situation where real and imagined worlds exist separately are termed 'perception studies', whereas those dealing with one common world consciously experienced are referred to as 'humanistic studies' (Kostinskiy 1989).

The image and perception studies refer to perceived or perceptual space. Their aim is to discover a cognitive organization of space on the basis of which individuals transform decisions into behaviour. Investigations have been concerned mainly with mental maps, showing how people evaluate different parts of their environment. Such maps for various parts of large cities have been elaborated by Barbash (1977, 1986) and Veshninski (1983, 1988). The former presented mental maps as related to the action spaces of individuals, showing how sets of urban elements were identified, about which people had information and attached to them subjective preferences. There were also studies, for example by Barbash (1981) and Butronenko (1981), which attempted to identify the latent characteristics (attributes) of urban territory and their influence on human behaviour. Privalov and Shvedov (1981), in turn, investigated how different social groups perceived the structure of particular fragments of an urban area. A number of studies were conducted by Kogan (1982) with respect to large Soviet cities. The studies dealt with the way in which people perceived the urban environment and the different ways they evaluated its various fragments.

Humanistic studies concern the environment surrounding human beings, perceiving it mainly as a 'cultural container' whose elements are of a symbolic or metaphoric character which create attitudes having the form of identity and attachment to place, or that of the sense of place (Kaganov 1981; Mikhailov 1983). In these studies the image of the environment in human consciousness is analysed and interpreted in terms of the attitudes and intentions people reveal with respect to the world within which they live. Such studies were originally carried out under the influence of psychologists and focused on the problem of how the spatial dimension influenced human awareness and behaviour. The work concerned the emotional and symbolic values that people attached to places (Kaganov 1981; Heidmets et al. 1979; Veshninski 1984), as well as the problem of human attitudes to places at a microscale, mostly a dwelling space and home territory where a specific form of territoriality arose (Heidmets 1980, 1981; Manuylov 1983; Pavlovskaya 1983). In recent studies on the sense of place an aesthetic element has been added. To identify a specific language in which the environment is being described and assessed, a semiotic approach has been applied (Rossinskaya 1989; Gabidulina 1989). The aesthetic aspects have also been analysed with respect to peculiar forms of the environment, for example to a totalitarian one (Rapaport 1989). There were investigations on place identity using a qualitative approach (Vanagas 1987), and studies of the concept of social role which created characteristic types of behavioural environments inscribed into the urban landscape (Savchenko 1989).

Recently, work has appeared dealing with the world outside the urban scene. Fedulov (1988) studied the image of the rural environment as it appeared in the consciousness of the inhabitants of small villages, as well as attitudes resulting from feelings of a sense of place.

Way of life in a broad sense

Each of the three kinds of studies presented above has dealt with one of the major aspects of what has been defined earlier as way of life in a broad sense. The complexity of this phenomenon means that studies have been concerned mostly with particular components rather than with the entire concept. There have, however, been some attempts to investigate way of life in a more comprehensive form. Among these attempts have been two studies involving all three aspects mentioned earlier: living conditions, activity and consciousness. The first of these studies was by Raitviir (1979), the second by Fedulov (1988). Their main aim was to identify the classes or categories within the concept of way of life using the above components as criteria. The first study concerned the population of the Estonian Republic; the second dealt with the rural population of the Moscow district. The difficulties encountered when all three components are considered caused the investigations to be limited to two aspects. Within this type of research two major kinds of enquiries can be distinguished: ethnosociological studies and those on migration behaviour.

In ethnosociological investigations into way of life, two aspects are combined, that of consciousness and that of activity. The everyday life and activity of ethnic groups is examined, and the focus is on the particular characteristics defining this life. The studies concern either an individual ethnic group (Lauristin 1984; Kasperovich 1985), or more than one group, mostly two occupying the same area (Koloskov 1984; Smotrikovskiy 1984; Boshkov and Golofast 1985; Starovoytova 1987). Recently, research has addressed the problem of ethnic conflicts (Afonov 1988; Saidov 1988). Studies of migration largely involve interaction between living conditions and consciousness. The latter is interpreted in terms of either migration preferences or ethnic awareness. Migration preferences are taken into account when movement from the countryside to urban areas is analysed

(Zaslavskaya 1981; Yevteeva 1987), or when studying the problem of potential migrants (Atayan and Novikov 1986). The factor of ethnic consciousness, on the other hand, is considered when the migration of national minorities is studied (Ivanov 1986; Shklaev 1986; Subbotina 1988).

Local communities

The concept of local community, as applied in contemporary Soviet social geography, has its roots in the notion of the territorial group introduced earlier by Kabo (1947). The concept was given contemporary form in the 1980s, mainly under the influence of sociologists who emphasized the social aspects of the phenomena rather than the environmental ones as geographers did earlier (for example, Goryachenko et al. 1978).

There are various definitions of local community in Soviet literature. Although they vary, there are five common elements which they share. Petrov (1983), Shkaratan (1986) and Shmirnyagin (1989) enumerate these as follows: (1) local community is a social formation historically created and in the process of continuous development – it emerges within society independently of the will and consciousness of people, and is conditioned by particular socio-economic relations characteristic of this society; (2) local community is a category that involves all the elements and relations of social structure of the society – economic, productive, technico-organizational, cultural, ideological etc. – because of which it operates as a relatively independent social organism; this relative independence implies a certain gap which can be completed only within the framework of the whole society, meaning that the local community is a link in the societal structure, connected with other links by a variety of relations; (3) local communities form a hierarchical structure in which those lying lower in the ladder enter into the composition of those lying higher; (4) local communities differ as to the degree of their distinction with regard to the surroundings (other communities), and (5) the basic function of local community is the continuous socio-demographic reproduction of its members.

Only recently have studies started to grasp the empirical aspects of the local community concept, and to date two phenomena have been investigated: (1) that of the nature of links ensuring group coherence (the problem of the nature of local community), and (2) that of the ethno-cultural aspects of social reproduction within the local community.

The problem of the nature of bonds within local community structure is analysed primarily with regard to small-scale social groups occupying urban territory. This type of study is known in the literature as an environmental approach (Mikhailov and Paadam 1986; Vanagas 1987; Mulla 1988; Paadam 1988). According to it, the environment is a local community comprising a group of families living as a rule within a housing estate. They present a mosaic of socio-economic and cultural characteristics that form a specific social environment (structure) to which individuals tend to adapt. The process of adaptation involves not only individuals, but also whole families. Living in the same area they constitute a common adaptive environment. This means that, for every family, the remaining ones (creating its immediate neighbourhood) form the environment which the family exploits and to which it adapts. The common adaptive environment is, however, a precondition to the constitution of a local group. Neighbourhood bonds, shaped in this environment, are merely the initial conditions for such a group to emerge. The group is created by generations, more exactly by neighbourhood relations based on genera- tion bonds. These bonds originate between generations, both within a family and within the same generation groups in the neighbourhood terri- tory. Local community as a collection of families living in a common territory and bound by neighbourhood-generation relations produces a new type of environment within which the process of individuals' socialization takes place. Adaptation and socialization reinforce the bonds grouping people together in territorial wholes. The group of families constitute the structure which enables, and at the same time constrains, individual behaviour. This behaviour consists in adaptation to the social environment through the process of socialization, during which individuals modify and change the structure, influencing and reshaping the relations occurring within it.

Within the studies of territorial groups, research has recently emerged concerning the rural environment, using a humanistic approach (Fedulov 1988). Rural communities have been investigated in terms of the concept of a primary community, understood as an informal social group charac- terized by certain attributes, such as a degree of self-consciousness of its members, informal social control, specific moral and social values, feelings of autonomy and attachment, and an awareness of a unique structural organization. Various combinations of these attributes help to distinguish different types of local rural communities. Studies of ethnocultural aspects of social reproduction within the local community have only recently developed. An example is work by Shkaratan (1986) on urban communities. Following Bromley (1973), Shkaratan considers a culture, and within it, an urban culture, as having two aspects. The first takes the form of a collection of facts related to a variety of cultural activities forming often separate, non-connected elements; these are an external indication of certain deeper conditions. The second aspect comprises meanings attached to cultural phenomena. These meanings are latent and difficult to catch at first sight. Grasping them needs intuition, feeling and aesthetic sensibility. It is these meanings that constitute a fundamental component of culture, and without them it is impossible to understand the latter. In every social group, behaviour and reactions to external stimuli are conditioned by meanings characteristic of the culture, which are generally accepted and obligatory. As Shkaratan suggests, it is useful to apply the hypothesis of cultural core to elucidate these meanings. The cultural core is related to the phenomenon of local community; it comes into being as a result of the integration of the cultural aspects of the major spheres of activity within this community. More precisely, the cultural core is a common fragment of productive, socionormative, cognitive, service and consumptive functions, as well as being the ultimate aim of all these functions. The aim is an extended, quantitative and qualitative reproduction of the social group which represents this culture. Reproduction is achieved through optimal adaptation to a particular socio-historical and natural circumstance within which the group is situated.

According to Shkaratan, one or more cultural cores may exist within the local community. It depends on the number of ethnic groups constituting local society. The character of the core, its structure and content, depends also on the functional structure of the local (urban) community (the more complex the latter, the more complicated the structure of the core); on changes in the size of population created by the intensity of reproduction processes and migration exchange, and on the physical characteristics of the local environment. According to Shkaratan, one of the fundamental components of the cultural core of a particular ethnic group is the family, within which the process of self-reproduction occurs, as well as cultural traditions, customs, behavioural norms and respect to society, of which the family is an element.

Conclusions

Social geography in the Soviet Union has a long tradition dating back to the studies undertaken in the last decades of the nineteenth century. With the emergence of the Soviet system, a new paradigm was introduced which seized the discipline, stifling study for many years. Social geography revived gradually only during the 1970s and developed considerably in the last decade. Basic research fields were formed at that time and valuable studies emerged. These studies have been discussed in terms of the major problems being analysed and the frameworks of ideas being applied.

6

Conclusions

Introduction

The second half of 1989 will go down in history as the beginning of probably the largest social revolution in Europe this century. The process of revolutionary change which originated then has now spread over more than half the territory of the continent, a territory inhabited by many different nations. Perhaps this is why many specialists sometimes call the autumn of 1989 the 'autumntide of nations'.

The changes that started then have lasted until now, producing new facts and events all the time. The fundamental attribute of these changes has been their ubiquity. They have concerned literally every sphere of life. The stream of events has been all-embracing, complicated in its course, full of changes, differing tendencies, contradictory phenomena and paradoxical solutions. The brief description presented below of what is now occurring in Eastern Europe and the former Soviet Union deals with events and changes in the most important spheres of life: politics and ideology, the economy, and social and cultural areas. This description is the starting point for considerations of how current, profound changes in the life of the region are reflected in geographical literature and of what the most probable direction is in the evolution of human geography in the region in the near future.

In the sphere of politics and ideology, changes in the region consisted in rejecting, first in Eastern Europe and then in the countries of the Soviet Union, the idea of the ruling role of the Communist Party. Communist parties as the centres of ideology for internal and external politics have been abolished, and at the same time control over domestic and international opinion as well as the distortions of economic development have ceased. New formations have developed instead, which have established new, democratic governments open to the rest of Europe. The monopoly of one ideology, one political formation, and the monopoly of the state bureaucracy over decisions about the economic lives of countries have been abandoned. Material possibilities for safe human rights have emerged through the rationalization of the economy, the reduction of state ownership, the facilitation of private enterprise and the emergence of democratic rights. The rules guiding the economies of the countries in the region have started to become similar to rules in the rest of Europe. This has created the basis for broadening economic and technical co-operation between both parts of the continent. At the same time, the asymmetrical, imperialist character of international relations in Eastern Europe has ceased to exist. A new, symmetrical and democratic system of relations has gradually emerged. As a result, within the region new subregional, political structures have developed embracing different groups of nations, for example the Warsaw–Prague–Budapest triangle.

In the sphere of the economy, the new political climate has made it possible to develop economic relations of a quite different character from before. In general, most of the countries in the region have accepted a capitalistic system as a model for the development of their own economies. In order to achieve this model the process of privatization, both of the means of production and of financial capital, has begun. New, previously unknown institutions of economic life have gradually developed and new relations have emerged in the economic structure of the countries in the region. One of the most important goals of the new governments has been to make national currencies convertible and to establish an elastic and appropriate system of economic law in order to attract both international and domestic capital. The process of modernizing national economies according to the rules of a capitalistic model is relatively slow, however. It depends, to a large extent, on the stimulation of western capital, which is needed for investment in Eastern Europe and the Soviet Union. What prevents this is the still anachronistic economic system in these countries. Most of the means of production there are still in the hands of the state bureaucracy. The banking system and the telecommunication infra-structure, which should facilitate and protect the circulation of financial capital, are underdeveloped. At the same time the impoverished population is unable to establish the conditions for prosperous enterprises, and there are still many problems with regulating the juridical issues relating to the economic system. With the exception of the market for consumer goods there is no existing market for investment goods, the market for capital is very poor and the market for labour is still unstructured.

All this means that the fundamental goal which governments in the region pursue is the restructuring of their economies by the transformation of branch, territorial and proprietary structures. The realization of this transformatory process is a precondition for initiating the development of a healthy economy which can ensure the growth of the level of satisfaction of social needs and the increase of productive potential.

What has happened to ideology, politics and the economy is reflected in the social life of the region. Together with the process of deep ideological and political transformations, and with the process of privatization, the uniform and to a large extent undifferentiated social structure inherited from the previous system has been subject to fast erosion. New social groups and classes have emerged, and differences among them have been increasing in terms of social position and living standards. The rapid growth of unemployment and of the number of people living in poverty has been unprecedented. Unemployment has chiefly been the result of the liquidation of unprofitable factories. It has not been absorbed locally, as the process of closing old factories has not been accompanied by the creation of new jobs.

In the countries where the process of social diversification and the increase in the gap between rich and poor is most advanced, there is social protest against the changes that are taking place. Poland, where the changes have been going on the longest, can serve as a good example. Here, the last parliamentary elections (November 1991) revealed a prejudice not reported so far against the process of change (fewer than 50 per cent of voters took part in the elections) and a wish to return to the previous system which is often considered to be socially more just (the communists won second place in the elections). Social resistance to the reforms is not conducive to the accomplishment of economic change, and poor economic achievements in turn intensify social disappointment. The lack of social support produces at the same time particular political consequences. In Bulgaria, Romania and many of the Soviet republics the communists still enjoy the confidence of a large part of society and this means that the process of change in these countries proceeds at the slowest pace, and people still remain in the chains of communism. A conviction prevails there, supported by the results of the shock therapy applied in other countries – i.e. the adaptation to a capitalistic model – that the latter is a greater evil than communism.

Perhaps the most spectacular and often most tragic phenomena in the current history of the region have occurred on the border of two spheres of life – the social sphere and the cultural sphere. These are the phenomena related to the problems of national and ethnic minorities. Communism produced a specific system of relations which was conducive to the mainte-nance of ethnic tensions without any possibility of applying any measures to relieve these tensions. The separateness and grading of people according to their ethnic dissimilarities was always accentuated. Now, in the new conditions mutual claims and animosities have been released. They have appeared most often in the form of accusations aimed at particular ethnic groups for errors and incorrectnesses in social life while under communist rule. If economic and territorial claims are added, it may easily lead to the outbreak of conflicts. Current examples are Yugoslavia and some Soviet republics. On the basis of national discords, nationalisms easily arise which intensify the problem. National conflicts are the most important factor destabilizing the current political situation in the region.

A cultural phenomenon of perhaps the largest dynamic and scale is the revival of religion in the countries of Eastern Europe and the republics of the Soviet Union. Communism fought against religious life in all possible ways, beginning with administrative methods and ending with economic ones. In all the countries of the region, except for Poland, an all-embracing process is occurring of rapid sacralization of social life. This process is the stronger, the more repressive the authorities were in the past with regard to the church. The number of believers has been increasing rapidly as well as the number of baptisms. Informal movements and religious communities have been forming. Religion has slowly become a privileged conveyor of moral and cultural values. The religious renaissance is conducive to the development of national languages, in many republics of the Soviet Union for example, and at the same time is a strong factor dynamizing nationalisms. This process does not occur by itself, but is strongly interrelated with other aspects of the current process of change in the region, especially the political aspect. The church takes part more and more in political life. More and more members of the clergy are entering into the composition of political institutions. Christian parties are arising in numbers that produce a complex political mosaic in the region.

Literature in the region in the context of contemporary changes

The events and processes presented above have their spatial dimension. It is this dimension that should be examined by geographers. The question thus arises whether the process of change which has been taking place in Eastern Europe and the former USSR for more than two years, and specifically the territorial aspect of this process, is reflected in the geographical literature on the region.

It is not easy to answer this question explicitly as the period of two years is too short, at least from the point of view of the needs of the procedure of publishing. In most of the countries in the region this procedure takes approximately two years. And even if geographers had immediately started examining the process of change from its very beginning, the first published results should appear in the second half of 1991 at the earliest, taking into account the time required to collect data and interpret it. This is confirmed in practice. Excluding Poland and the USSR, no publications appeared in the region in 1990 concerning the problem of contemporary changes. The first works, of which there are few, were published in 1991.

The literature produced in 1990 and 1991 can be divided into two groups. On the one hand, there are works which are continuations of studies conducted earlier, i.e. before 1990. These have appeared only in Poland. On the other hand, there are studies which have only recently become concerned with the problem of contemporary changes in the region. So far, only four works of this kind have been published, one each in Czechoslovakia, Hungary, Poland and the Soviet Union. These two groups of research are discussed in turn.

Studies before 1990

Current studies in Poland on the process of contemporary changes are the continuation of a piece of work which started far earlier, at the beginning of the previous decade. This was a study concerning the problem of the socio-economic crisis and its spatial consequences under the conditions of the communist system. Investigations into the crisis of Polish space started in 1981 and continued until the break in 1989. At that time, in the remaining countries of the region this type of survey was not carried out. It was officially recognized that there were no crises. Only in Poland, where a disastrous social and economic situation brought about deep social upheaval and provoked the emergence of the Solidarity movement, did the conditions exist for carrying out a study of the crisis and its spatial aspects.

Very generally speaking, the results of the study showed that in Poland, apart from the spatial differentiation of crisis phenomena, there was also a crisis of space resulting from particular activity with regard to the space itself which was understood as a specific, limited good. The crisis of space took the form of contradictions which were caused by the disproportions produced during the process of the socio-economic transformation of space. These were structural disproportions connected with different methods of land use and different ways of using land resources as instruments of economic, social and even ideological policy. These functional disproportions and related contradictions were revealed in various spheres, or in other words, were characteristic of different kinds of space.

The study distinguished between five such kinds of space: (1) political space, whose problematics comprised primarily the territorial organization of the country; (2) economic space, related to the spatial organization of economy; (3) social space, concerning the problem of the social infra-structure as well as the problem of the polarization of social structures and the foundations of social perception and aspirations; (4) cultural space, and (5) physical space, from the point of view of the utilization of natural resources and of environmental conditions.

For the purposes of the study of the formation of functional dispro-portions and of the course of the crisis within the above spaces as well as within the national space (their synthesis), geographers attracted specialists from other social disciplines to co-operate. The aim of the study was to produce a diagnosis of the existing state of affairs, to identify the underlying factors and to seek for ways out.

At the beginning, the study was concerned with problems at a macrolevel dealing with spatial units on a mainly regional and supraregional scale as well as on a national scale. From the year 1986 onwards, studies in microscale emerged dealing with the issue of local communities from the viewpoint of the contradictions appearing within the communities and with the course of the crisis phenomena on a local scale. As in the case of the investigations carried out in macroscale, the analysis conducted in microscale concerned phenomena and processes in the political sphere (the structure of political and administrative authorities, their strategy and functioning as well as the relations between the authorities and local society); in the economic sphere (the structure of key branches of the local economy and their relationship with supralocal economic systems); in the social sphere (social attitudes, social structures and disparities, social orientations, social consciousness, traditions and personality), and in the cultural sphere (the culture of national minorities, the place and role of culture in social life, professional culture). The results of the study were published mainly in two series: in the *Biuletyn Komitetu Przestrzennego Zagospodarowania Kraju* (Bulletin of the Committee for the Spatial Organization of the Country) beginning from 1981, and in the *Rozwoj regionalny – rozwoj lokalny – samorzad terytorialny* (Regional development – local development – territorial self-government) which started to appear in 1986. As the former was concerned primarily with phenomena and processes at the macrolevel, the latter dealt with the problems taking place on a local scale.

The study of the crisis phenomena in space and of the crisis of the space itself enriched geographical knowledge with new experiences and with new developments in the areas of theory and methodology. What was most important, however, was that this knowledge proved very useful in the study of the phenomena and processes that emerged later as a result of contemporary changes in the country.

Contemporary studies in the region

Investigations have started recently both in Poland and in other countries of Eastern Europe. The Polish studies are discussed first, followed by those produced in Czechoslovakia, Hungary and the Soviet Union.

The studies now being carried out in Poland on the process of contemporary change are the continuation of the crisis geography in at least three aspects. Firstly, these investigations are conducted by the same group of specialists in geography and other social sciences who developed the geography of crisis. Although new titles are being produced and new topics developed, the authors remain mostly the same. Apparently, the geographers who have not pursued investigations before 1990 on the crisis of Polish space lack the proper experience to change their attitudes in order to cope with new problems. Secondly, the idea of the investigations remains the same; this is Polish space and its condition as a consequence of the political, economic and social processes which are taking place within it. Thirdly, the study is continued at two levels of territorial aggregation – the macrolevel which refers to spatial units on regional and larger scales, and the microlevel which comprises investigations on a local scale.

What is new in contemporary studies is the completely different nature of the phenomena under investigation. The essence of the changes which are now occurring in Poland is the subordination of the process of socio-economic development to the rules of the market mechanism. Political processes are strongly correlated with this mechanism. In order to inculcate this mechanism as quickly as possible, the process of restructuring the economy is necessary. This economy is still embedded by its roots in the previous era, and without restructuring no social and economic revival is possible.

The process of restructuring has its spatial determinants and consequences, and these are of main interest to geographers studying Polish space in the new political, economic and social conditions. At present, the investigations concern, on the one hand, the process of restructuring on a local, regional and national scale, and on the other hand, the problems of local communities. The problem of restructuring is discussed first, followed by the current study concerning local communities.

The problem of restructuring comprises three main types of investigations: (1) theoretical studies; (2) case studies of certain regions of Poland and the possibilities of their development in the context of European co-operation, and (3) other empirical studies dealing with various determinants of the process of the restructuring of Polish space. Most of the work is published in *Studia regionalne i lokalne* (Regional and local studies) which are the continuation of the earlier mentioned series *Rozwoj regionalny – rozwoj lokalny – samorzad terytorialny*, and now edited by the European Institute of Regional and Local Development at Warsaw University.

Theoretical studies refer to both those factors and determinants of the process of restructuring which are the results of the process of spatial organization, and to methods of managing space and the territorial organization of the country. One of the most important here is the issue of state intervention in the management of space, that is, the degree to which the central authorities may interfere in the plans for the spatial organization of regions. The present, liberal-democratic policy of the state rejects the possibility of constructing plans for the restructuring of space on the scale of the whole territory of the country (state regional plans). This produces a number of drawbacks, mainly in terms of the cost of reforming the existing spatial structure of social and economic life in the country. Important also is the question of recessive (problem) areas. They cover a considerable part of the country. For the needs of restructuring, the problem of unemployment should first be resolved – now the main social soft-spot, and the element which is destabilizing economic life. As a way out of the situation a transfer of labour power to the better developed areas is being proposed which should be conducive to their further development, but the housing question is of primary significance. Without its resolution it is impossible to transfer manpower to other regions. This is thus not an issue of a merely social character as many planners think, but an indispensable factor of economic development (Jalowiecki 1991).

Very important to the problem of the structural transformation of socio-economic life in Poland is the implementation of a proper model for the territorial organization of the country. This should be the model which produces the best conditions for developing a civic society and a social market economy based on the decentralized organization of the state, but with mechanisms which are able to balance different and often contradictory problems. The model should take into account a multi-level hierarchical spatial structure which accords with the historically developed structure of the territorial organization of the country as well as with the contemporary requirements of socio-economic development (Kolodziejski 1991).

Much attention is dedicated to the role of self-government institutions and their relationships with central organizations. Connected with this is the problem of the optimal division of powers between local and central levels. An example of this kind of study is Warsaw, whose new system of self-government is gradually paralysing the functioning of the city (Jalowiecki 1991).

Theoretical studies also deal with the nature of Polish space. This space is discontinuous in the sense that at least three kinds of areas can be distinguished within it: regions with good chances for development, declining regions, and intermediate regions. This division made it possible to undertake empirical investigations on several different regions chosen from among the three categories. The investigations concerned the problem of reconstruction and regional development from the point of view of incorporating the Polish economy into the European system. They form the second group of studies within the restructuring approach. Their purpose is to describe and explain; (1) the present state of the economy and social life; (2) the origin of this state, and (3) the ways the past state of the economy and social life have determined their present state and their future situation. This is the basis for constructing: (1) the plan of development for a region to be adapted to the conditions of the modern European economy, which takes into account the trump cards of regional economy, and (2) the plan for restructuring the regional economy which enables its desirable state to be achieved as quickly and effectively as possible (Wojtasiewicz 1991).

The third group is the study dealing with the problem of the restructuring of certain chosen areas on both a regional and a local scale. The study refers mainly to declining regions. The largest among the investigations concerned the process of reconstruction of the economy and social life of the Upper Silesia region (Nawrocki 1991; Szczepanski 1991). This process requires many-sided decisions and activity in the political, economic and social spheres. An optimal variant is the mobilization of the population of the region based on wide self-governing autonomy, together with strong support from the central authorities. This support takes the form of capital and investment costs, proper legal policies and policy in the sphere of qualified personnel assistance. Effective restructuring requires the consolidation of regional authorities, the reconstruction of the regional political system, and the weakening of the regional bureaucracy connected with the mining-industrial lobby. In social life, it is necessary to restore the cultural and social identity of the region, as well as to liberate internal factors of development. It is also necessary to reconstruct the educational system. The subject of the reconstruction processes should be the human individual and the local community.

An important part of the investigations concern the local scale. Of interest here is the study of poles of growth and stagnation. It results from the study that growth poles are urban places with long historical traditions performing important, subregional functions; where the industrialization processes have not destroyed the architectural tissue, and where a middle class and middle-class traditions have survived. In these types of urban places there is a dynamic increase in enterprise and privatization processes. The opposite situation is found in those settlement units which originated and developed on the basis of industrialization processes; which have an immigrant population with little experience of urban life, and where there is no middle class.

There are also investigations which concentrate primarily on the local scale and deal with the phenomenon of local communities. These investigations developed earlier, particularly during the 1980s. Their current objective is the social and political situation in local areas in connection with the elections of 1989. The analysis refers to the changes which took place in the time before the elections to the senate and parliament in June 1989. There was considerable animation of the local political scene and entirely new forms emerged of spontaneous social activity not controlled by the authorities. A leading role was played by civic committees which during the electoral campaign appointed many new leaders. After the elections, at the beginning of 1990, civic committees became the most powerful element in local political scenes, playing an important role in organizing all aspects of the life of local communities (Jalowiecki 1991).

Another large study concerns the problem of how territorial local governments perform their duty a year after the elections. The analysis covers about 250 *gminas* (the smallest administrative units) – a sample of more than 10 per cent of all the *gminas* in Poland. Various aspects are examined of local self-government in operation, among others the problem of new people in the authorities, the structure of local political scenes, major actors on these scenes, the social practices of local authorities and their economic policies (Jalowiecki and Swianiewicz 1991).

The studies described above present, in principle, the whole output on the problem of spatial analysis of the consequences of the contemporary political, social and economic changes in the country. As has been mentioned earlier, these studies exhaust almost entirely not only what has been written in the Polish literature, but also in the literature of other countries in the region. Apart from this output, there are only four items published by geographers from the region which deal with the spatial aspects of the contemporary changes in this part of the continent. These are works of geographers from Poland, the Soviet Union, Czechoslovakia and Hungary.

The work of the Polish geographer Rosciszewski (1991) refers to Eastern Europe and is a discussion of the criteria for the delimitation of the region, taking into account the problems related to the changes since

1989. This is a geopolitical work outlining political, historical, economic and social processes, the result of which is the formation of a third socio-economic space in the area between Western Europe and the former Soviet Union, a space which is different from the adjoining regions. Particular attention is paid to contemporary events and the impact they exert on the situation in the region. Emphasis is laid on the problem of the geopolitical situation of the area and the issue of national minorities.

In the Soviet literature, there has so far appeared only one study which signals the interest geographers attach there to the problem of the changes that are taking place in the former USSR. These are the proceedings of the ninth conference of the Soviet Geographical Society which was held in November 1990 in Kazan (Abramov *et al.* 1991). Such a conference is organized every five years and, as the authors emphasize, this was the first meeting in the period of *perestroika* under conditions of *glasnost* and democratization. Apart from the plenary session, the debates took place in the form of six round-table meetings. Among them only one was devoted to social and economic problems. The most important issues for the contemporary situation of the country were discussed: the relations among national minorities and ethnic groups; geographical aspects of economic reforms; the problem of planning territorial development under the new conditions, and that of improving the territorial organization of the country.

The interest of geographers from Czechoslovakia and Hungary has been in the parliamentary elections and their spatial aspects. In Czechoslovakia this problem has been studied by Blazek and Kostelecky (1991). They present the spatial distribution of votes with reference to the main political parties, and the social and economic structure of voters; they discuss the differences among the parties from the point of view of their electoral achievements.

In Hungary, Kovacs (1991) has applied a broader approach. He has examined Hungarian electoral law with special emphasis on its geographical and historical aspects, and analysed the spatial pattern of voters' participation and the support given to political parties during elections.

The evolution of human geography in the region in the immediate future

As is seen from the above review, geographers in Eastern Europe and the Soviet Union have so far been interested only in a fragment of what is now occurring in reality. Little work has yet been done on spatial studies of even the most spectacular phenomena in the region, which are the national problems and conflicts. Little more attention has been focused on processes in the social sphere or on the economy. There is also a considerable lack of analysis of cultural phenomena in space. A relatively large amount of work has only been done with regard to political events and processes. Thus, most of the human geography in the region is still engaged in studying problems which have no connection with contemporary events taking place in this part of the continent, and only a few geographers have decided to tackle the new phenomena. What, then, will the immediate future look like as regards the subject matter of the discipline, and what will be the most probable direction of its evolution?

The changing reality undoubtedly exerts a strong impact on the problems which geographers are going to study in the near future. The first results should be observable soon, although too little time has passed to estimate how many geographers are following the current changes. At the same time these changes are happening so fast that it will take a long time to study all their aspects. Even if the process of change ends and the situation becomes stabilised, the adaptation of the discipline to the new reality will last for some time to come. Nevertheless, the process of the restructuring of human geography in Eastern Europe and the former Soviet Union has already started. This is an objective process, and more and more geographers will take part in it to cope with the problems produced by the changing reality. It seems that the present decade will see the most intensive changes in the discipline. Not only will its subject matter alter, but also its nature will change, which will have consequences in creating the need to look for new theoretical approaches and methodological solutions. This will be because the present theoretical and methodological capabilities of the discipline will soon prove insufficient to face the current massive changes in the surrounding world. These changes are taking place simultaneously in all spheres of life, and the spatial aspects produce very complex mosaics. Studying these mosaics will require more methods and theories, and they will be borrowed from modern economics, sociology, cultural studies and political science now being developed in the west. When everything changes at the same time, as is the case in Eastern Europe and the former Soviet Union, a complex, multidisciplinary approach is required to grasp all the aspects which are needed in the analysis. An example of such an approach has been given by Polish geographers who conducted the research work simultaneously on four basic spaces (political space, social space, economic space and cultural space) using two scales of spatial analysis – microscale and macroscale – and attracting many specialists from different social sciences. This model of enquiry should soon become prevalent in other countries, if only by virtue of the traditionally good contacts among geographers in the region.

At the same time, a considerable opening up to western geography will take place. Western geography has a far longer tradition of co-operating with other social sciences. This can be a good model to follow for geographers from the east of Europe. In western geography, subdisciplines have developed which have still not been applied by geographers from the eastern part of the continent. Examples of these are financial geography, the geography of marketing and markets, the geography of gender, political geography, the geography of culture and the geography of national minorities. Their development in Eastern Europe and the former USSR is indispensable in order to comprehend new phenomena which are now occurring in the region. The incorporation of these and similar subdisciplines will speed up the reconstruction of human geography in this part of the continent and the process of its becoming more similar to western geography.

This process of reconstruction for internal and external reasons will probably not spread evenly in time and space across the region. There are at least three factors responsible for such a situation which we can call the historical factor, the factor of potential, and the political factor.

The historical factor is the development of human geography up till now and its current condition in particular countries of the region. As the review above indicates the differences among the countries are substantial. The most advanced in the process of disciplinary reconstruction is human geography in Poland. Here, much earlier than in other countries, the subject matter and methodology of human geography were adapted to the needs of description and explanation of those crisis processes which brought about the breakdown of the old system and the new emerging reality. The remaining national human geographies started later in their attempts to grasp the changing world around them; their histories of studying contemporary processes are far shorter than in Poland, and they have a smaller research output. One can say that the process of restructuring human geography in Czechoslovakia, Hungary and the former USSR has just started. The first studies are appearing; their content, however, is selected accidentally and there is no idea of a complex approach to reality similar to that produced by the Polish geographers.

In the geographical literature of the three remaining countries, Bulgaria, Romania and Yugoslavia, there is no work dealing with contemporary changes in the subregion. Human geography there is still not able to adapt to the changing reality, and the process of its reconstruction has not yet started.

The factor of potential is very roughly related to the number of academic research workers in particular countries. The presence of a substantial number of researchers, is essential for the reconstruction of the discipline, since with a large number of research centres the effect of self-stimulation takes place – it is easier to develop interdisciplinary contacts, the field of research analysis broadens more quickly, new disciplines arise more quickly and new methods are better adapted. From this point of view the best situation is in the former Soviet Union where the number of academic centres and research workers surpasses considerably that of the remaining countries taken together. A large scientific potential is an important factor in the further development of the discipline and one should expect that in a short time, perhaps in this decade, there will appear in the former Soviet Union the largest number of studies dealing with the contemporary changes. The potential of Polish human geography can be estimated at second in the region. The traditions of disciplinary development and the large output already produced allow us to presume that Polish geography will play a considerable role in the development of the discipline in the region. The remaining countries present much smaller potentials than these two. The development of human geography and the level of its reconstruction is differentiated, however. Czechoslovakia and Hungary are more advanced, whereas geographers from Bulgaria, Romania and Yugoslavia have not yet started to make structural changes in their research fields.

Without doubt, the political factor in this case may prove decisive. The destabilized political situation in Bulgaria and Romania, as well as the tragic events in Yugoslavia, are unfavourable for the evolution of the discipline in these countries. A new human geography open to the problems and changes in the surrounding world will start only when changes take place which enable the establishing of a fully democratic way of life.

Bibliography

Abramov, L. S., Alayev, E. B., Antipova, A. V., Kolosov, V. A., Koronkevich, N. I., Shlikhter, S. B. 1991: Itogi IX Sezda Geografiche skogo Obshchestva SSSR (The Ninth Congress of Geographical Society of the USSR). *Izvestia Akademii Nauk SSSR, ser. geog.* 2, 5–21.

Ackerman, E. A. 1958: Geography as a fundamental research discipline. University of Chicago, Department of Geography Research Paper 53.

Afonin, Y. I. 1988: K voprosu o prichinakh negativnykh yavleni v natsyonalnykh otnosheniakh i putyakh ikh ustranenia (On the question of the reasons for negative phenomena in national relations and ways of their elimination). In Chuprov, V. I. and Ivanov, V. N. (eds.), *Puti sovershenstvovania sotsyalisticheskogo obraza zhizni v period perestroyki*, Moscow: Institut Sotsyologicheskikh Issledovani AN SSSR, 66–7.

Afonin, Y. I. 1988: O prichinakh negativnykh yavleni v nacionalnykh otnosheniakh (About negative issues in the relations among different nationalities). *Tezisy Konferencji, Kishinov.* Moscow: VLKSM, 13–15.

Agafonov, I. T. 1984: O sushchnosti i osnovnykh zadachakh sovetskoy sotsyalnoy geografii (About the essence and fundamental tasks of Soviet social geography). *Izvestia vsesoyuznogo geograficheskgo obshchestva,* 116, 205–11.

Aganbegian, A. G., Bagrinovski, K. A. and Granberg, A. G. 1972: *Sistema modelei narodnokhoziaistvennogo planirovania* (The system of models of planning of the national economy). Moscow: Mysl.

Alayev, E. B. 1980: Perspektivy razvitia sotsyalno-ekonomicheskoy geografii na sovremennom etape (Perspectives on development of socio-economic geography in the contemporary period). *Geografia i prirodnye resursy* 3, 154–9.

Alayev, E. B. 1982: Ekonomicheskaia i sotsialna geografia-struktura i obshche tendencii (Social Geography – the structure and general tendencies). *Itogi Nauki i Tekhniki* 16, 7–21.

Alayev, E. B. 1983: *Sotsyalno-ekonomicheskaya geografia: terminologicheski slovar* (Socio-economic geography: a terminological dictionary). Moscow: Mysl.

Alexandrovskaya, O. A. 1982: Vasili Nikitich Tatishchev, 1686–1765. *Geographers' Bio-Bibliographical Studies*, 129–32.

Alexandrovskaya, O. A. 1982a: Mikhail Vasilevich Lomonosov, 1711–1765. *Geographers' Bio-Bibliographical Studies*, 65–70.

Alekseyev, A. I. 1983: Sotsyalnye aspekty razvitia geosystem (Social aspects of the developments of geosystems). In *Dinamika geograficheskikh sistem*, Moscow, 70–6.

Alekseyev, A. I. 1984: Zhizn naselenia kak predmet sotsyalnoy geografii (Life of people as the subject matter of social geography). *Voprosy geografii* 123, 77–85.

Alekseyev, A. I. and Kovalev, S. A. 1987: Sotsyalno-geograficheskiye issledovania v sovremenny period razvitia strany (Socio-geographical studies in the contemporary period of development of the country). *Vestnik Moskovskogo Universiteta, ser. geogr.* 3, 3–8.

Alekseyev, A. N., Bozhkov, O. B. and Glukhov, V. D. 1975: Obraz zhizni, sotsyalnaya differentsyatsya, gorodskaya obshchnost (Way of life, social differentiation, urban society). In *Planirovaniye sotsyalnogo razvitia gorodov*, Moscow: Institut Sotsyologicheskikh Issledovani AN SSSR, 128–53.

Anokhin, A. A. and Kostyayev, A. I. 1980: Nekatorye napravlenia sotsyalnoy geografii (Some developments in social geography). In *Regyonalny ekonomiko-geograficheski analiz*, Frunze: Kyrgystan, 28–38.

Anokhin, A. A. and Fedorov, T. M. 1984: Sotsyalna geografia v sistemie nauk (Social geography in the system of sciences). *Vestnik Leningradskogo Universiteta, ser. geogr.* 18, 102–5.

Anuchin, V. A. 1960: Teoreticheskie osnovy geografii (Theoretical foundations of geography). Moscow: Mysl, 254 pp.

Anuchin, V. A. 1960: *Teoreticheskaya geografia* (Theoretical geography). Moscow: Mysl.

Atayan, L. N. and Novikov, V. M. 1986: Territorialnaya obshchnost i vyavlenie osnovani sposobov formirovania sotsyalnoy aktivnosti lichnosti (Territorial community and its effects on the social activity of an individual). In *Vosproizvodstvennye mekhanizmy goroda v uslovyakh intensyfikatsii regionalnogo razvitia*, Tallin: Tallinski Politekhnicheski Institut, 119–20.

Babicz, J. 1978: Wincenty Pol, 1807–1872. *Geographers' Bio-Bibliographical Studies*, 93–8.

Balans vremeni naselenia Latviyskoy SSR. 1976, Riga: Zinatne.

Bandman, M. K. 1971: Podkhod i osnovnye etapy reshenia zadach optimizacii formirovania TPK (An approach and main stages in optimizing the process of formation of TPC). In *Modelirovanie formirovania TPK*, Novosibirsk.

Bartosiewiczowa, S. and Czarniecka, I. 1968: Daily commuting to work. *Geographia Polonica* 13, 101–21.

Baranskiy, M. N. 1980: *Stanovlenie Sovietskoy ekonomicheskoy geografii, Izbrannye trudy*. (The establishment of Soviet economic geography. Selected works). Moscow: Mysl.

Barbash, N. B. 1977: Opyt issledovania faktornoy ekologii Moskvy (Factorial ecology studies of Moscow). In *Gorodskaya sreda i puti eyo optimalizatsii*, Moscow: Institut Geografii AN SSSR, 37–53.

Barbash, N. B. 1981: Znanie goroda kak indikator otnoshenia naselenia k razlichnym elementam sredy (Knowledge of the city as an indicator of the attitude of inhabitants to different elements of urban environment). In *Chelovek i sreda-psikhologicheskiye aspekty*, Materialy konferencji v Lohusalu, Tallin, 181–4.

Barbash, N. B., Gimpelson, V. V. and Davidovich, Y. A. 1985: Opyt sotsyalnogo kartirovania goroda Moskvy (Social mapping of Moscow). *Sotsyologicheskiye issledovania* 4, 75–83.

Barbash, N. B. 1986: *Metodika izuchenia territorialnoy differentsyatsii gorodskoy sredy* (The method of studying the territorial differentiation of the urban environment). Moscow: Institut Geografii AN SSSR.

Barbash, N. B. and Raitviir, T. 1986: Sravnitelnaya faktornaya ekologia krupnykh gorodov (Comparative factorial ecology of large cities). In *Vosproizvodstvennye mekhanizmy goroda v usloviakh intensifikatsii regionalnogo razvitia*, Tallin: Trudy Politekhnicheskogo Instituta, 91–3.

Bartkowski, T. 1988: Miejsce zamieszkania jako jeden ze stymulatorow patriotyzmu lokalnego (The place of residence as a stimulus of a local patriotism). *Rozwoj Regionalny-Rozwoj Lokalny-Samorzad Terytorialny*, 13, 69–90.

Bartosiewiczowa, S. and Czarniecka I. 1966: Daily commuting to work. *Geographia Polonica* 13, 101–21.

Basuk – in Romanowski J. 1971: East-Central and Southeast European agriculture. In: Hoffman G. W. (ed.) *Eastern Europe: essays in geographical problems*. London: Methuen, 126–57.

Batakliev, I. 1938: Istorija na zaselvaneto i formy na seliscata (The history of settlement process and the forms of settlement) *Trud. na Statist. inst. za stop. Proucv*. 2–3.

Beba, B. and Murawska H. 1985: Male mlasto w badaniach etnograficznych (Ethnographic studies of a little town) *Etnografia Polska*, 29, vol. 1, 77–84.

Beluszky, P. 1965: A classification of rural settlements in Hungary. *Foldrajzi Ertesito* 14, 149–63 (in Hungarian).

Beluszky, P. 1966: The central hierarchy of urban settlements in the Great Plain. *Foldrajzi Ertesito* 15, 329–45.

Berezowski, S. (ed.) 1969: *Geografia Ekonomiczna Polski* (Economic Geography of Poland). Warsaw: PWN.

Berg, L. S. 1962: *Istoria russkikh geograficheskikh otkriti* (The history of Russian geographical discoveries). Moscow: Izd-vo Akademii Nauk SSSR.

Bernstein-Kogan, S. V. 1924: *Ocherki ekonomicheskoi geografii* (Essays in economic geography). Moscow: Gosizdat.

Beshkov, A. S. and Valev, E. B. 1961: *Geografia na Bulgaria 2*. Sofia: Bulgarska Akademia na Naukite.

Bialas, J. 1982: Zachowania mieszkancow a przestrzen spoleczna osiedla (The behaviour of inhabitants and the social space of a neighbourhood). In Pioro, Z. (ed.) *Przestrzen i Spolecznestwo*, Warsaw: Ksiazka i Wiedza, 304–11.

Blazek, J. and Kostelecky, T. 1991: Geograficka analyza vysledku parlamentnich voleb v roce 1990 (The geographical analysis of the results of parliamentary elections in 1990). *Sbornik Ceskoslovenske Geograficke Spolecnosti* 1, 1–14.

Blazhko, N. I. 1976: Teritorialne sistemy i ikh modelirovanie (Territorial systems and their modelling). In *Matematicheskie metody w geografii*, Kazan: Izd-vo Kazanskogo Universiteta.

Blaskovic, V. 1967: *Ekonomska geografija Jugoslavije* (The economic geography of Yugoslavia). Zagreb: Informator.

Bora, D. 1961: Nekatorye problemy issledovania ekonomicheskikh rajonov v Vengrii (Some research problems in the field of economic regionalization of Hungary). *Prace Geograficzne* 27, 61–77.

Boros, F. 1967: The association between the size of settlement and the supplying functions. *Foldrajzi Ertesito* 16, 239–50 (in Hungarian).

Bozhkov, O. B. and Golofast, V. B. 1985: Otsenka naselenyem uslovi zhizni v krupnykh gorodakh (The quality of life as evaluated by inhabitants of large cities). *Sotsyologicheskiye issledovania* 3, 95–101.

Bromley, Y. V. 1973: *Ocherki teorii etnosa* (The outline of the theory of ethnos). Moscow: Mysl.

Buga, D. 1967: Contributions to the studies of the geography of the Danube delta population. *Comunicari de Geografia* 8, 95–105 (in Romanian).

Burton, I. 1963: The quantitative revolution and theoretical geography. *The Canadian Geographer* 7, 151–62.

Buttimer, A. 1971: *Society and milieu in the French geographic tradition*. Chicago: Rand McNally.

Buttimer, A. 1987: Edgar Kant, 1902–1978. *Geographers' Bibliographical Studies* 71–82.

Butronenko, V. N. 1981: Vtorichnye svoystva territorii, ikh vospriyatie i uchet v proyektirovanii gorodov (Secondary characteristics of a territory, their perception and significance in urban design). In *Chelovek i sredapsikhologicheskiye aspekty*. Tallin: Materialy konferentsii v Lohusalu, 181–4.

Buttner, M. and Jakel, R. 1982: Anton Friedrich Busching, 1724–1793. *Geographers' Bio-Bibliographical studies* 7–16.

Byudzhet vremeni gorodskogo naselenia (The time budget of the urban population), 1976. Moscow: Statistika.

Chernyshevski, N. G. 1949: *Polnoe sobrane sochineniy* (Collected works). Moscow: Gosizdat.

Chojnicki, Z. and Dziewonski, K. 1978: Podstawowe zagadnienia metodologiczne rozwoju geografii ekonomicznej (Fundamental methodological problems of the development of economic geography). *Przeglad Geograficzny* 50, 205–11.

Cholnoky, J. 1910: Die Oberflachengestalt des Alfold. *Bull. Hungarian Geogr. Soc.*: Internatl. Edit., 38, 275–97.

Cotet, P. 1979: Alexander-Dimitrescu Allen, 1880–1917. *Geographers' Bibliographical Studies* 35–8.

Culik, F. 1966: The structure of settlements in CSSR and the possibility of selecting appropriate centers. *Acta Geographica Universitatis Comenianae* 6, 303–18.

Cvijic, J. 1918: The zones of civilization of the Balkan Peninsula. *Geographical Review* 8, 345–61.

Demangeon, A. 1962: The origins and causes of settlement types. *Readings in Cultural Geography*, Chicago: University of Chicago Press, 506–16.

Dick, N. E. 1965: Mikhail Vasilevich Lomonosov i ego znachenie dla ekonomicheskoi geografii (M. V. Lomonosov and his contribution to economic geography). In: Baranski N. N. (ed), Ekonomicheskaia geografia v SSSR. Moscow: *Prosveshchenie*, 258–65.

Dinev, L. and Velchev, I. 1965: Geographical distribution, structure and problems of population in the district of Pazardzhik. *Godishnik na Sofiskia Universitet* 59, 151–221.

Dinev, L. 1966: Obecny stan i przyszle zadania geografii ludnosci i osadnictwa v Bulgarii (Present status and future tasks of the geography of population and settlement in Bulgaria). *Przeglad Geograficzny* 38, 199–204.

Dobrolubov, N. A. 1936: *Polnoe sobranie sochinieni* (Collected works). Moscow: Gosizdat.

Dobrowolska, T. 1985: Wiez lokalna (Local social link) *Etnografia Polska* 29, vol. 1, 59–64.

Dolenko, A. V. and Savinov, L. I. 1986: Sostoyanie i territoryalnaya mobilnost gorodskogo naselenia (Social and territorial mobility). In *Problemy sotsyologii regiona*, Saransk: Minvu, 40–9.

Dolinin, A. A. 1975: Sotsyalna geografia – osobaya vetv geografii naselenia (Social geography – a separate branch of population geography). In *Teoreticheskiye aspekty ekonomicheskoy geografii*, Leningrad: Izdatelstvo Geograficheskogo Obshchestva SSSR, 53–61.

Dolinin, A. A. 1976: Sotsialna geografia – osobaya vetv geografii naselenia (Social geography – a distinct branch of population geography). In: Teoreticheskie aspekty ekonomicheskoi geografii). *Leningrad. Izd. G. O. SSSR*, 53–61.

Domanski, R. 1978: *Ksztaltowanie otwartych regionow ekonomicznych* (The formation of the open economic regions). Warsaw: Panstwowe Wydawnictwo Ekonomiczne.

Dyoniziak, B., Mikulowski-Pomorski, J. and Pucek, Z. 1978: Wspolczesne spoleczenstwo polskie (The contemporary Polish society). Warsaw: *Panstwowe Wydawnictwo Naukowe*, 255.

Dziewonski, K. 1956: Geografia ludnosci i osadnictwa (The geography of settlements and population). *Przeglad Geograficzny* 28, 723–64.

Dziewonski, K. 1961: Theoretical problems in the development of economic regions. *Regional Science Association Papers* 8.

Dziewonski, K. 1962: Procesy urbanizacyjne we wspolczesnej Polsce (Urbanistic processes in contemporary Poland). *Przeglad Geograficzny* 34, 459–508.

Dziewonski, K. 1967: Teoria regionu ekonomicznego (The theory of economic region) *Przeglad Geograficzny* 39, 33–49.

Dziewonski, K. and Leszczycki, S. 1960: Geographic studies of economic regions in Central Eastern Europe. *Przeglad Geograficzny* 32, Supplement, 109–13.

Dziewonski, K. and Kosinski, L. 1965: Changes in the distribution of population in Poland. *Geographia Polonica* 7, 69.

Dziewonski, K. and Wrobel, A. 1961: Raboty po ekonomicheskomu rajonirovaniu v Polshe (Studies of division of Poland into economic regions). *Prace Geograficzne* 27, 93–104.

Enyedi, G. 1961: Eine Methode fur die Abgenzug von landwirtschaftlichen Rayons (A method for delimiting agricultural regions). *Prace Geograficzne IG PAN* 27, 285–93.

Enyedi, G. 1967: The agriculture of the world. *Abstracts*, Hungarian Academy of Sciences, 9.

Enyedi, G. 1984: South-East Europe. In: Johnston R. J. and P. Claval (eds.) *Geography since the Second World War: an international survey*. London-Sydney: Croom-Helm, 64–78.

Esakov, V. A. 1978: Dmitry Nikolaevich Anuchin, 1843–1923. *Geographers' Bio-Bibliographical Studies* 1–5.

Esakov, V. A. 1980: Vasily Dokuchaev, 1882–1945. *Geographers' Bio-Bibliographical Studies* 33–42.

Eyles, J. 1984: The examination of social relationship in space: its territorial, empirical and practical parameters. *GeoJournal* 9, 247–53.

Evteeva, N. V. 1987: Kto i pochemu vozvrashchayetsa v selo? (Who returns to the countryside and why?). *Sotsyologicheskiye issledovania* 2, 61–4.

Freeman, T. W. 1966: *The geographer's craft*. Manchester University Press.

Freeman, T. W. 1967: *The geographer's craft*. Manchester University Press, Barnes and Noble, New York.

Friganovic, M. 1962: The population of the coastal zone of Sibenic. *Geografski Glasnik* 24, 1–38 (in Serbo-Croat).

Gabidulina, S. E. 1989: Psikhosemanticheskiy podkhod k izucheniu gorodskoy sredy (Psychosemantic approach to the study of urban environment). In Vysokovskiy, A. A. and Kagonov, G. Z. (eds.), *Gorodskaya sreda*, Moscow: Institut Teorii Arkhitektury i Stroitelstva, 2, 42–51.

Gerasimov, I. 1976: *A short history of geographical science in the Soviet Union*. Moscow: Progress Publisher.

Ghegheshidze, A. M. 1982: Teritorialna organizatsya kachestva sredy v sotsyalno-ekonomicheskikh kompleksakh (Territorial organization of the quality of the environment in socio-economic complexes). In *Voprosy izuchenia okruzhayushchey sredy*, Tbilisi, 92–105.

Gherasimov, I. B. *et al.* (eds.) 1960: *Monografia geografica Republicii Populare Romine*. Bucuresti: Editura Akademiei.

Gieorgica, J. and Dutkiewicz, P. 1988: Stosunek aparatu administracji panstwowej do reform politycznych (The attitude of the state administration workers to political reforms). *Rozwoj Regionalny-Rozwoj Lokalny-Samorzad Terytorialny* 11, 85–118.

Gochman, V. M. 1979: Obshchestnennaya geografia – sushchnost i struktura (Social geography – its essense and structure). In *Izuchenie problem sotsyalno-ekonomicheskoy i sotsyalnoy geografii*, Tartu: Materialy nauchnogo soveshchania, 45–58.

Goncev, G. 1938: Izcesznalite selisca v Bolgarija (The declining places in Bulgaria). *APP. g. 1, kn.* 1, 38–55.

Gordon, L. A. and Klopov, V. 1972: *Chelovek posle raboty: sotsyalnye problemy byta i vnerabochego vremeni* (Man after work: social problems of life and leisure). Moscow: Nauka.

Goryachenko, E. E., Zaslavskaya, T. I. and Krapchan, S. G. 1978: Differentsyatsya sotsyalno-demograficheskogo sostava zhiteley selskikh poseleni Siberi (Social and demographic differentiation of rural population in Siberia). In *Puti sotsyalnogo razvitia derevni*, Novosibirsk, 28–41.

Gould, P. 1982: *The geographer at work*. London: Routledge and Kegan Paul.

Grano, O. 1979: Johannes Gabriel Grano, 1882–1956. *Geographers' Bio-Bibliographical Studies* 73–84.

Halamska, M. 1989: Czynniki roznicujace dynamike zachowan w spolecznosciach lokalnych (Factors differentiating the dynamics of behaviour in local communities). *Rozwoj Regio nalny-Rozwoj Lokalny-Samorzad Terytorialny* 20, 206–28.

Haufler, V. 1966: Changes in the geographical distribution of population in Czechoslovakia. *Rozpravy Ceskoslovenske Akademie Ved* 76.

Haufler, V. 1967: Changes in the geographical distribution of population in Czechosolovakia, *Rozp. Ceskoslov. Akad. Ved* 76, 8–38.

Heidmets, M. 1980: Sotsyalno-psikhologicheskie problemy zhiloy sredy – aspekty personalizatsii sredy (Socio-psychological problems of housing environment – aspects of personalization of environment). In Heidmets, M. (ed.), *Chelovek, sreda, obshchenie*, Tallin: Izdatelstvo Pedagogicheskogo Instituta, 39–45.

Heidmets, M. 1981: Sredovye komponenty chelovecheskogo 'ya' – problemy dla psikhologii i arkhitektury (Environmental components of the human 'I' – problems for psychology and architecture). In *Chelovek i sreda – psikhologicheskie aspekty*, Tallin: Materialy konferentsii v Lohusalu, 130–1.

Heidmets, M., Kruusvall, Y. and Kulgas, P. 1979: Obshchenie v obshchestvennom tsentre (Personal relations in the city centre). In Heidmets, M. (ed.), *Chelovek, sreda, prostranstvo*, Tartu: Tartuski Gosudarstvenny Universitet, 82–99.

Hooson, D. J. M. 1968: The development of geography in pre-soviet Russia. *Annals AAAG* 58, 250–72.

Hryniewicz, J. Zroznicowanie podstaw spoleczno-politycznych w zaleznosci od miejsca zamieszkania (The differentiation of socio-political attitudes in relation to the place of residence). *Rozwoj Regionalny-Rozwoj Lokalny-Samorzad Terytorialny* 21, 229–52.

Humboldt and Ritter – in James and Martin (1981, pages 112–131). Czirbusz – in Joerg W. 1922: Recent geographical work in Europe. *Geographical Review* 12, 431–84.

Hurski, E. 1962: The territorial development of Czechoslovak towns. *Sbornik Ceskoslov. Spolecnosti Zemepisnc* 70, 41–54 (in Czech).

Iskierski, J. 1989: Kaszubskie spolecznosci lokalne – warianty przemian (Cashubian local communities – the ways of evolution). *Rozwoj Regionalny-Rozwoj Lokalny-Samorzad Terytorialny* 20, 274–301.

Ivanicka, K. (ed.) 1964: *The geography of the region of East Slovakian ironworks*. Bratislava: Slovak Pedag. Publisher.

Ivanov, V. P. 1986: Etnicheskie osobennosti migratsii selskogo naselenia Chuvashskoy ASSR (Ethnic peculiarities of the migration of rural population in Chuvash ASSR). In *Sovremennye etnosotsyalnye protsessy na sele*, Moscow: Materialy konferntsii Kazan 1983, 204–8.

Jalowiecki, B. 1980: Czlowiek w przestrzeni miasta (Man within an urban space). Katowice: *Slaski Instytut Naukowy*, 227.

Jalowiecki, B. 1982: Proces waloryzacji przestrzeni miejskiej (The process of evaluation of urban space). In: Pioro Z. (ed.) *Przestrzen i spoleczenstwo* (Space and society). Warsaw: Ksiazka i Wiedza, 64–112.

Jalowiecki, B. 1986: Social geography in Poland. In: Eyles J. (ed.) *Social geography in international perspective*. London and Sydney: Croom Helm, 172–84.

Jalowiecki, B. 1990: Narodziny demokracji w Polsce (The birth of democracy in Poland). *Rozwoj Regionalny-Rozwoj Lokalny-Samorzad Terytorialny* 25, 169.

Jalowiecki, B. 1991: Uwarunkowania restrukturyzacji polskiej przestrzeni (The determinants of restructuring the Polish space). *Studia Regionalne i Lokalne* 4 (37), 13–40.

Jalowiecki, B. and Swianiewicz, P. (eds.) 1991: Miedzy nadzieja a roz czarowaniem. Samorzad terytorialny w rok po wyborach (Between hope and disappointment. Territorial self-government a year after the elections). *Studia Regionalne i Lokalne* 3 (36), 218p.

James, P. E. and Martin, G. J. 1981: *All possible worlds: A history of geographical ideas*. New York: John Wiley and Sons.

Johnson, R. J. 1983: *Geography and geographers:Anglo-American human geography since 1945*. London: Edward Arnold.

Johnson, R. J. 1986: North America. In: Eyles J. (ed.) *Social geography in international perspective*. London and Sydney: Croom Helm, 30–59.

Kabo, P. M. 1947: Priroda i chelovek v ikh vzaimnom otnoshenii kak predmet sotsyalno-kulturnoy geografii (Nature and man in their mutual interplay as the subject matter of socio-cultural geography). *Voprosy geografii* 5, 5–32.

Kaganov, G. Z. 1981: Vospriyatie prostranstvennoy sredy naselenyem istoricheskogo goroda – na primere Leningrada (The perception of the spatial environment by inhabitants of a historic city – the case of Leningrad). In *Chelovek i sreda – psikhologicheskie aspekty*. Tallin: Materialy konferentsii v Lohusalu, 173–6.

Kaganski, V. L., Polyan, P. M. and Rodoman, B. B. 1980: V. P. Semenov-Tyan-Shanski's region and country: its present day relevance and meaning. *Soviet Geography* 21, 355–63.

Kania, C. 1963: Problematyka miejsc centralnych w bylym Regierungbezirk Oppeln (The problem of central places in the former Regierungsbezirk Oppeln). *Materialy i Studia Opolskie* 4, 95–9.

Kania, C. 1966: Metoda analizy 'rank-and-size' na przykladzie wojewodztwa Opolskiego (Method of analysis 'rank-and-size' on the example of the voivodship Opole). *Czasopismo Geograficzne* 37, 311–23.

Karpukhin, A. and Kuznetsova, N. 1979: Ratsoyonalny byudzhet vremeni trudyashchikhsia i problemy yego dostizhenia (Rational time budgets of the working people and problems of their attainment). *Ekonomicheskie nauki* 9, 51–9.

Kaser, M. 1967: *COMECON: Integration problems of the planned economies*. London and New York: Oxford University Press.

Kasperovich, G. I. 1985: Migracla naselenia v gorod i etnicheskie processy (Migration to urban place and ethnic processes). Minsk: *Nauka i Tekhnika*, 149.

Khachatryants, K. K. 1981: Zhilishche i obraz zhizni (Dwelling and way of life). *Stroitelstvo i Arkhitektura Bielorussii*, 4, 12–14.

Kielczewska, M. 1931: Osadnictwo wiejskie Wielkopolski (The rural settlement in Great Poland). *Badania Geograficzne Uniwersytetu Poznanskiego*, Poznan.

Kielczewska, M. 1937: L'evolution cyclique d'habitat rural etiude dans la Pomeranie. *C. Congres Intern. de Geogr. Varsovia 1934*, 3, Warsaw.

Kielczewska-Zalewska, M. 1964: Rozwoj badan geograficznych osadnictwa wiejskiego w Polsce (Evolution of geographical research on rural settlements in Poland). *Czasopismo Geograficzne* 6, 352–73.

Kirilov, 1727: In: Nikitin, N. N. 1966: A history of economic geography in pre-revolutionary Russia. *Soviet Geography* 7.

Kish, G. 1987: Paul Teleki, 1879–1941. *Geographers' Bibliographical Studies* 139–44.

Klichyus, A. 1974: *Metodika obsledovania byudzhetov vremeni naselenia malykh gorodov* (Methods of investigating the time budget of the population of small urban places). Vilnius: Zataga.

Kogan, L. B. (ed.) 1982: *Sotsyalno-kulturnye funktsii goroda i prostranstvennaya sreda* (Socio-cultural functions of the city and the spatial environment). Moscow: Stroyizdat.

Kolodziejski, J. 1991: Polityczno-administracyjne aspekty restrukturyzacji regionow (Political and administrative aspects of the problem of restructuring the regions). *Studia Regionalne i Lokalne* 4 (37), 115–52.

Koloskov, Y. D. 1984: K voprosu issledovania territorialnykh razlichy v sotsyalnom potrebleni (About the study of spatial differentiation in social consumption). In *Prikladnye sotsyalno-geograficheskie issledovania*, Tartu, 198–202.

Kolossovski, N. N. 1958: Proizvodstvenno-Territorialnye Sochetanie v Sovetskoi Ekonomicheskoi Geografii (Territorial-production complex in the Soviet Economic Geography). *Osnovy Ekonomicheskogo Raionirovania*.

Kondracki, J. 1981: Stanislaw Lencewicz, 1899–1944. *Geographers' Bio-Bibliographical Studies* 77–82.

Konstantinov, O. A. 1961: Geograficheskie issledovania gorodov v SSSR (The geographical study of urban places in the USSR). *Materialy k pervomu mezhduvedomstvennomu soveshchaniu po geografii naselenia*, 3, Moscow–Leningrad.

Kosinski, L. 1963: Procesy ludnosciowe na Ziemiach Odzyskanych (Demographic processes in the recovered territories). *Prace Geograficzne* 40.

Kosinski, L. 1967: *Geografia ludnosci* (Geography of population). Warsaw: Panstwowe Wydawnictwo Naukowe.

Kostinski, G. D. 1989: Obraz cheloveka i ustanovki soznania v issledovanii gorodskoi sredy (The concept of man in studying urban space). *Gorodskaja sreda: Sbornik materialov konferencji arkhitektov, Suzdal 1989.* Moscow, 42–48.

Kostrowicki, J. (ed.) 1965: Land utilization in East-Central Europe. Case studies. *Geographia Polonica* 5, 512.

Kostrowicki, J. 1966: Zdjecie uzytkowania ziemi i jego przydatnosc praktyczna (The land use survey and its practical utility). *Biuletyn Komitetu Przestrzennego Zagospodarowania Kraju* 42, 211–15.

Kostrowicki, J. 1967: *Monografia wojewodztwa Bialostockiego* (The monography of the Bialystok voivodship). Lublin: Wydawnictwo Lubelskie.

Kovacs, Z. 1991: Az 1990 evi parlamenti valasztasok politikai foldrajzi tapasztalatai (Political geographical implications of the 1990 Hungarian parliamentary elections). *Foldrajzi Ertesito* 1–2, 55–81.

Kovalev, S. A. 1966: Geografia potreblenia i geografia obsluzhivania naselenia (Geography of consumption and geography of services). *Vestnik Moskovskogo Universiteta ser. geogr.* 2, 37–49.

Kovalev, S. A. and Pokshishevskiy, V. V. 1967: Geografia naselenia i geografia obsluzhivania (Population geography and geography of services). In *Nauchnye problemy geograf naselenia*, Moscow: Izdatelstva Moskovskogo Universiteta, 34–47.

Kostinski, G. D. 1989: Obraz cheloveka i ustanovki soznania v issledovanii gorodskoy sredy (The image of man and approaches to mental perception in studies of the urban environment). In Vysokovski, A. A. and Kaganov, G. Z. (eds.), *Gorodskaya sreda*, Moscow, Institut Teorii Arkhitektury i Stroitelstva, 1, 42–9.

Krivokapic, B. 1966: Contemporary geographical social transformations in urban and suburban zones of Niksic. *Geografski Preglad* 10, 121–32 (in Serbo-Croat).

Kruber, A. A. 1923: *Obshchye zemlevedenie* (General geography). Moscow: Gosizdat.

Kuklinski, A. 1967: Kryteria lokalizacji zakladow przemyslowych (Criteria for locating industrial plants). *Biuletyn Przestrzennego Zagospodarowania Kraju* 45, 140.

Kuklinski, A. 1984: Uspiony potencjal (A dormant potential). *Zycie Gospodarcze* 13.

Lappo, G. M. 1981: Problemy ispolzovania narodnokhozaystvennogo potentsyala bolshikh gorodov na sovremennom etape ekonomicheskogo i sotsyalnogo razvitia SSSR (Problems of the utilization of national-economic potential of large cities in the contemporary stage of economic and social development of the USSR). *Izvestia Akademii Nauk SSSR. ser. geogr.* 3, 11–21.

Lauristin, M. 1984: Priobshchenle k kulture v poseleniakh raznogo typa Estonskoi SSR (The attachment to culture in the settlement units of various types in the Esthonian SSR) *Tezizy Dokladov minara, Tartu. Izd.* Tartus. Univer. 128–31.

Lauristin, M. 1986: Problemy integratsii naselenia goroda kak sotsyalnoy obshchnosti (Problems of integration of urban population as asocial group). In *Vosproizvodstvennye mek hanizmy goroda v usloviakh intensifikatsii regionalnogo razvitia*, Tallin: Trudy Politekhnicheskogo Instituta, 100–11.

Lauristin, M., Kruusvall, Y. and Raitviir, T. 1975: Regionalnoe, sotsyologicheskoe issledovania obraza zhizni (Regional sociological study of way of life). *Planirovanie sotsyalnogo razvitia* 2, 154–75.

Lavrov, S. B. and Sdasyuk, G. V. 1980: *Sovremennaya ekonomicheskaya i sotsyalnaya geografia* (Contemporary economic and social geography). Moscow: Znanie.

Lavrov, S. B., Anokhin, A. A. and Agafonov, N. T. 1984: Sotsyalnaya geografia – problemy stanovlenia nauchnogo napravlenia (Social geography – problems of forming a scientific orientation). In *Sotsyalnaya geografia v SSSR: problemy metodologii i teorii*, Leningrad: Geograficheskoe Obshchestvo AN SSSR, 3–13.

Lebedev, D. M. 1952: Iz istorii ekonomicheskoi regionalizacji Rossli (From the history of economic regionalization of Russia). *Izviestia Akademii Nauk SSSR, ser. geogr.* 3.

Lenin, V. I. 1932: Polnoye sobranie sochinieni (Complete works). Moscow.

Leonhard-Migaczowa, H. 1965: Podstawowe problemy ludnosciowe wojewodztwa wroclawskiego ze szczegolnym uwzglednieniem struktur demograficznych (Basic demographic problems of the Wroclaw voivodship with particular reference to demographic structures). *Acta Unversitatis Wratislaviensis* 34.

Leszczycki, S. 1937: Les types de l'habitat rural dans la Pologne du Sud-Ouest. *C. R. Congres Intern. de Geogr. Varsovie 1934.*

Libura, H. 1988: Badania wyobrazen geograficznych na przykladzie mieszkancow Sanoka (Surveying mental images: the case of Sanok). *Dokumentacja Geograficzna* 1, 90.

Lijewski, T. 1967: Dojazdy do pracy w Polsce (Commuting to work in Poland). *Studia KPZK* 15.

Lis, A. G. 1975: On the question of the composition of economic territorial complexes (a critique of Kolossovski's technological cycles). *Soviet Geography* 15, 20–7.

Lis, A. G. 1977: On the question of the composition of economic territorial complexes (a critique of Kolosovski's technological cycles). *Soviet Geography* 18, 20–27.

Loczy, L. (ed.) 1919: A geographical, economic and social survey of Hungary, Budapest.

Macka, M. 1964: On methodological problems of studies on daily commuting to work. *Zpravy o vedecke cinnosti* 3.

Maiminas, E. Z. 1971: *Procesy planirovania v ekonomike* (Planning processes in the economy). Moscow: Mysl.

Manuylov, Y. S. 1983: Personalizatsya sredy kollektivom kak factor vospriyatia yego lichnosti (Personalization of environment by the group as a factor in perception of its individuality). In Niit, T., Heidmets, M. and Kruusvall, J. *Psikhologia i arkhitektura*, Tallin: Tallinski Pedagogicheski Institut, 32–9.

Marinov, K. 1961: Ekonomiko-geograficheskie issledovania po ekonomicheskomu rajonirovaniu v Bolgarii (Economic-geographical investigations in the field of economic regionalization in Bulgaria). *Prace Geograficzne* 27, 15–30.

Maryanski, A. 1963: Wspolczesne migracje ludnosci w poludniowej czesci pogranicza polsko-radzieckiego (Contemporary migrations in the southern part of the Polish–Soviet frontier). Cracow: Wyzsza Szkola Pedagogiczna.

Mechnikov, N. P. 1965: Civilization. In Nikitin, N. P. 1965c: Mechnikov L. I. Baranski N. N. (ed.), Ekonomicheskaia geografia v SSSR. Moscow: *Prosveshchenie*, 359–68.

Mehedinti, 1927: In Mihailescu, V. 1977: Simion Mehedinti, 1868–1962, *Geographers' Bio-Bibliographical Studies*, 65–72.

Mereste, V. I. and Nommik, S. V. 1984: *Sovremennaya geografia: voprosy teorii* (Contemporary geography: theoretical problems). Moscow: Mysl.

Mihailescu, V. 1977: Simion Mehedinti, 1868–1962. *Geographers' Bio-Bibliographical Studies* 65–72.

Mikhailov, D. R. 1983: Gorod kak sistema: organism ili sreda? (City as a system: organism or environment?). In Niit, T., Heidmets, M. and

Kruusvall, J., *Psikhologia i arkhitektura*, Tallin: Tallinski Pegagogicheski Institut, 19-24.

Mikhailov, D. R., Paadam, M. and Mulla, E. 1986: Sredovoe vzaimovlianie pokoleni v protsesse sotsyalizatsii (Environmental interdepedence between generations in the process of socialization). In Mikhailov, D. R. (ed.), *Vosproivodstvennye protsessy goroda*, Tallin: Valgus, 47-68.

Mikulowski-Pomorski, J. 1989: Polska prasa lokalna w swietle problematyki wiezi spolecznej (Polish local press in the light of the problem of social bonds). *Rozwoj Regionalny-Rozwoj Lokalny-Samorzad Terytorialny* 18, 275-84.

Mironenko, N. S. 1988: Napravlenia sotsyalnoy geografii: distizhenia i zadachi (Trends in social geography: achievements and tasks). In *Geografia v Moskovskom universitete*, Moscow: Izdatelstvo Moskovskogo Universiteta, 198-204.

Mints, G. I. and Nepomnyatsi, A. S. 1979: *Tendentsi izmenenia byudzheta vremeni rabotayushchego naselenia Latviyskoy SSR* (Tendencies in changes of the worker's time budget in Latvian SSR). Moscow: Institut Sotsyologicheskikh Issledovani AN SSSR.

Mrazkowna, M. 1922: Z antropologii Ziemi Krakowskiej (About the anthropology of Krakow District). *Przeglad Geograficzny*, 2, 105-27.

Mulla, E. 1988: K voprosu o formirovanii dispozitsyonnoy struktury lichnosti podrostkov v gorodskoy srede (About the formation of the dispositional structure of the adolescent's personality in the urban environment). *Trudy Tallinskogo Politekhnicheskogo Instituta* 649, 145-56.

Murdych, Z. 1965: Problems of the zoning of population characteristics in Prague. *Zbornik Ceskoslovenske Spolecnosti Zemepisne* 67, 41-54.

Nawrocki, T. 1991: Spoleczne uwarunkowania restrukturyzacji Gorne go Slaska (The social determinants of restructuring the Upper Silesia region). *Studia Regionalne i Lokalne* 4 (37), 395-422.

Nikitin, N. P. 1965c: Mechnikov L. I. In: Baranski N. N. (ed.), Ekonomicheskaia geografia v SSSR. Moscow: *Prosveshchenie*, 359-68.

Nikitin, N. N. 1966: A history of economic geography in pre-revolutionary Russia. *Soviet Geography* 7, 3-36.

Nimigeanu, G. 1980: Constantin Bratescu. *Geographers' Bio-Bibliographical Studies*, 19-24. London, Mansell.

Nommik, S. V. 1979: Sotsyalno-ekonomicheskie prostranstvennye sistemy kak obrazovateli sredy (Socio-economic spatial systems as creators of the environment). *Uchenye zapiski Tartuskogo Universiteta* 490, 3-24.

Nommik, S. V. 1982: Sotsyalno-ekonomicheskaya geografia v sistemie obshchestvennykh nauk (Socio-economic geography in the system of social sciences). *Izvestia Akademii Nauk SSSR. ser. geogr.* 4, 98-106.

Nowakowski, J. 1934: *Geografia jako nauka* (Geography as a science). Warsaw: Trzaska, Evert i Michalski.

Nurek, S. 1982: Waloryzacja przestrzeni osiedli micszkaniowych (The evaluation of the space of housing estates). *Prace Naukowe Uniwersytetu Slaskiego w Katowicach*, 387, 159.

Ocovsky, A. 1969: Prehlad literatury a arst vyvoja geografie sidel v Bulharsku (The survey of literature and outline of the development of settlement geography in Bulgaria). *Geografski Casopis* 21, 159–68.

Ossowski, S. 1960: *Dziela* (Works). Warsaw: Panstwowe Wydawnictwo Naukowe.

Paadam, K. 1988: Differentsyatsya gorodskoy sredy sotsyalizatsii pokoleni (Differentiation of the urban socialization environment between generations). *Trudy Tallinskogo Poltechnicheskogo Instituta* 649, 127–44.

Palamarchuk, M. M. 1983: Obshchestvenno-teritorialny kompleks: teoreticheskaya kontseptsya (Socio-territorial complex: a theoretical approach). In *Teoreticheskie problemy geografii*, Leningrad: Tezisy dokladov 4 vsesoyuznoy konferentsii, Chernovtsy 1982, 21–4.

Pavlovskaya, E. E. 1983: Sotsyalno-psikhologicheskie aspekty formirovania predmetno-prostranstvennoy sredy gorodskikh pridomovykh teritori (Socio-psychological aspects of forming a spatio-material environment in communal territories). In Niit, T., Heidmets, M. and Kruusvall, J. *Psikhologia i arkhitektura*, Tallin: Tallinski Pedagogicheski Institut, 166–70.

Pawlowski, S. 1935: Osiedla wiejskie na Pomorzu pod wzgledem geograficzno-osadniczym i narodowosciowym (The rural settlement in Pomerania from the geographical-settlement and ethnic viewpoint). *Pamietnik Instytutu Baltyckiego* 23, Torun.

Pawlowski, S. 1938: Inwieweit kann in der Anthropogeographie von einer Landschaft die Rede sein. Comptes rendus d. Congr. Intern. d. Geogr., Amsterdam, Tome 2, Sec. 3a, 202–208.

Pawlowski, S. and Czekalski, J. 1937: L'habitat rural en Pologne. Essai de la synthese. *C. R. Congres Intern. de Geogr., Varsovie 1934*.

Piasecki, E. 1964: Ludzie swiata i etniczna jednosc obszarow (Peoples of the world and ethnic unity of the territories). *Czasopismo Geograficzne* 35, 73–85.

Pecsi, M. and Sarfalvi, B. 1964: *The geography of Hungary*. Budapest: Corvina Press.

Petrov, A. V. 1983: Teritorialnye obshchnosti lyudey kak obekt izuchenia sotsyalnoy geografii (Territorial communities as the object of social geography). *Izvestia vsesoyuznogo geograficheskogo obshchestva* 1, 72–8.

Pohl, J. 1935: Typy vesnicktch sidel v Cechach (The types of rural settlement in Bohemia). *Narodni Vestnik* 27, 5–55.

Pokshishevski, V. V. 1964: Content and basic tasks of population geography. In *Geografia naselenia SSSR. Basic problems*, Moscow: Nauka.

Pokshishevski, V. V. 1965: Raboty Lwa S. Berga imieyushchie ekonomichesko-geograficheskoe znachenie (The works of Lev S. Berg having economic-geographical significance). In Baranski, N. N. (ed.), *Ekonomicheska geografia v SSSR*, Moscow Izd-vo Prosveshchenie.

Popp, N. 1978: Georges Valsan, 1885–1935. *Geographers' Bio-Bibliographical Studies* 2, 127–32.

Potkanski, T. 1922: *Pisma posmiertne* (Posthumous essays). Cracow.

Privalov, M. E. and Shvedov, S. S. 1981: Urbanisticheskaya sreda i osobennosti eyo vospriyatia zhitelami razlichnykh gorodskikh rayonov (Urban environment and the peculiarities of its perception by inhabitants of different urban districts). In *Chelovek i sreda – psikhologicheskie aspekty*. Tallin: Materialy konferentsii v Lohusalu, 202–5.

Probst, J. G. 1972: *Lokalizacja przemyslu socjalistycznego* (The location of industry in the socialist countries). Warsaw: Panstwowe Wydawnictwo Ekonomiczne.

Raitviir, T. 1979: *Sotsyogeograficheskie issledovania obraza zhizni i ego elementov* (Sociogeographical studies of way of life and its components). Tallin: Trudy Politechnicheskogo Instituta.

Raitviir, T. 1984: Voprosy formirovania sotsyogeografii na styke geografii i sotsyologii (Formation of sociogeography on the border of geography and sociology). *Naukovedenie v nashi dni* 5, 73–83.

Rapaport, A. G. 1989: K estetike totalitarnykh sred (About the aesthetic of totalitarian environments). In Vysokovski, A. A. and Kaganov, G. Z. (eds.), *Gorodskaya sreda*, Moscow: Institut Teorii Arkhitektury i Stroitelstva, 1, 78–86.

Regent, T. M. 1980: Odno iz pervykh sotsyalno-geograficheskikh issledovani selskoy mestnosti v Rosii (One of the first socio-geographical studies of a rural site in Russia). *Vestnik Moskovskogo Universiteta, ser. geogr.* 6, 80–3.

Rivkina, R. V. 1979: *Obraz zhizni selskogo naselenia* (Way of life of rural population). Novosibirsk: Nauka.

Rivkina, R. V. 1983: Metodologicheskie voprosy regionalnogo prognozirovania obraza zhizni (Methodological problems of the regional prognosis of way of life). *Regionalnye sistemy* 2, 30–4.

Rivkina, R. V. 1985: Problemy struktury sotsyalnykh grup (The problems of the structure of social groups) *Regionalne Sistemy* 2, 30–36.

Rosciszewski, M. 1991: Europa Srodkowa i jej specyfikacja przestrzenna (Central Europe and its spatial specification). Unpublished manuscript.

Rossinskaya, E. I. 1989: Semyoticheskie modeli vosproyatia arkhitekturnoy sredy (Semiotic models of perception of the architectural environment). In Vysokovski, A. A. and Kaganov, G. Z. (eds.), *Gorodskaya sreda*, Moscow: Institut Teorii Arkhitektury i Stroitelstva, 2, 51–5.

Rukavishnikov, W. O. 1980: *Naselenie goroda: sotsyalny sostav, rassielenie, otsenka gorodskoy sredy* (Urban population: social structure, distribution, evaluation of urban environment). Moscow: Statistika.

Rykiel, Z. 1984: Geografia dialectica. Una perspectiva polaca (Dialectical geography. The Polish point of view). *Publicacions i edicions de la Universitat de Barcelona*, 120.

Saidov, M. 1988: O nekatorykh problemakh obraza zhizni natsyonalnykh menshenstv (About some problems of the way of life of national minorities). In Chuprov, V. I. and Ivanov, V. N. (eds.), *Puti sovershenstvovania sotsyalisticheskogo obraza zhizni v period perestroyki*, Moscow: Institut Sotsyologicheskikh Issledovania, 66–7.

Sarfalvi, B. 1964: The various mechanisms of the social restratification and regrouping of population. *Foldrajzi Ertesito* 13, 487–503 (in Hungarian).

Saushkin, Y. G. 1965: Semenov-Tyan-Shanski P. P. kak ekonomiko-geograf (Semenov-Tyan-Shanski P. P. as an economic-geographer). In: Baranski N. N. (ed.), Ekonomicheskaia geografia v SSSR. Moscow: *Prosveshchenie*, 349–58.

Saushkin, Y. G. 1966: A history of Soviet economic geography. *Soviet Geography* 7, 1–104.

Saushkin, Y. G. 1973: Ekonomicheskaia geografia: istoria, teoria, metody i praktika (Economic geography: a history, theory, methods and practice). Moscow: Mysl.

Saushkin, Y. G. 1977: *Geograficheskaya nauka v proshlom, nastoyashchem i busdushchem* (Geographical science in the past, present and future). Moscow: Mysl.

Saushkin, Y. G. 1980: Aspekty sovetskoy sotsyalnoy geografii (Aspects of Soviet social geography). *Voprosy geografii* 115, 17–24.

Saushkin, Y. G. and Smirnov, A. M. 1968: Geosistemi i geostruktury. *Vestnik Moskovkogo Universiteta, ser. geogr.* 5.

Savchenko, M. E. 1983: Gorod i ego prostranstvo (Urban space). *Psikhologia i Arkhitektura* 1, 17–19.

Savchenko, M. R. 1989: O svoystvakh arkhitekturnoy sredy (About the characteristics of the architectural environment). In Vysokovsky, A. A. and Kaganov, G. Z. (eds.), *Gorodskaya sreda*, Moscow: Institut Teorii Arkhitektury i Stroitelstva, 1, 49–54.

Sawicki, L. 1910 Rozmieszczenie ludnosci w Karpatach Zachodnich (The distribution of population in Western Carpathians). Cracow, 28.

Secomski, K. (ed.) 1974: *Spatial planning and policy: theoretical foundations*. Warsaw: Polish Scientific Publisher.

Semenov-Tyan-Shanski, V. P. 1980: Region and country, in Kaganski et al., *Soviet Geography* 21, 355–63.

Sharigin, M. D. 1984: Sovremenye zadachi sotsyalno-ekonomicheskoy geografii (The contemporary tasks of socio-economic geography). *Izvestia vsesoyuznogo geograficheskogo obshchestva* 116, 97–104.

Shkaratan, O. I. 1986: *Etnosotsyalnye problemy goroda* (Ethnosocial problems of the city). Moscow: Nauka.

Shklaev, T. K. 1986: Etnicheskie faktory sposobstvuyuschchie migratsiu selskogo naselenia Udmurdskoy ASSR (Ethnic factors promoting the migration of rural population in Urmud ASSR). In *Sovremennye etnosotsyalnye processy na sele*, Moscow: Materialy konferentsii, Kazan, 1983, 119–28.

Sieminski, W. 1989: Wartosc miejsca w literaturze pieknej. Lokalnosc i uniwersalizm (The sense of place in literature. Locality and universality). *Rozwoj Regionalny-Rozwoj Lokalny-Samorzad Terytorialny* 20, 325–42.

Smirnyagin, L. V. 1989: *Rayony SSHA – portret sovremennoy Ameriki* (Regions of the USA – the portrait of contemporary America). Moscow: Mysl.

Smotrikovski, V. I. 1984: Natsyonalnye osobennosti khozaystvenno-bytovoy deyatelnosti gorodskikh semey (National pecularities of everyday life activities of urban families). In *Prikladnye sotsyalno-geograficheskie issledovania*, Tartu, 139–41.

Smotrikovski, V. I. 1984: Nacionalno-bytovye osobennosti struktury khozaistvenno-bytovoi deiatelnosti ggordskikh semei (The pecularities of the everyday activity of urban families). *Prikladnye Socio-geograficheskie lssledovania*. Tartu, 190–93.

Stan, C. 1961: Ekonomicheskie rajonirovanie v Rumynii (Economic regionalization in Romania). *Prace Geograficzne* 27, 105–14.

Starovoytova, G. V. 1987: Etnicheskie grupy v sovremennom gorode (Ethnic groups in a contemporary city). *Rasy i narody: sovremennye etnicheskie i rasovye problemy* 17, 110–22.

Staszewski, J. 1960: *Pionowy rozklad ludnosci na swiecie* (Vertical distribution of world population). Warsaw: Panstwowe Wydawnictwo Naukowe.

Stepanov, A. V. 1983: Troistvennost ponyatia 'Gorodskaya sreda' (The triple character of the concept 'Urban environment'). In Niit, T., Heidmets, H. and Kruusvall, J., *Psikhologia i arkhitektura*, Tallin: Tallinskiy Pedagoicheskiy Institut, 3–10.

Stepanov, A. V. 1989: Sotsyalnaya rol kak sredoobrazny fenomen (Social role as an environment creating phenomenon). In Vysokovski, A. A. and Kaganov, G. Z., *Gorodskaya sreda*, Moscow: Institut Teorii Arkhitektury i Stroitelstva, 54–60.

Strida, M. 1961: La division economique du territoire de la Tchecoslovaquie (The problems of economic regionalization of Czechoslovakia). *Prace Geograficzne* 27, 31–50.

Subbotina, I. A. 1988: Migratsya russkogo naselenia v Gruzinskoy ASSR (The migration of Russian population in Georgian ASSR). In *Vsesoyuznaya sesia po itogam etnograficheskikh i antropologicheskikh issledovani*, Sukhumi: Tezisy dokladov, 38–43.

Szczepanski, M. 1991: Kulturowe uwarunkowania restrukturyzacji Gornego Slaska (The cultural determinants of restructuring the Upper Silesia region). *Studia Regionalne i Lokalne* 4 (37), 363–94.

Tajti, F. 1956: Changes in the development of dispersed settlements and their population. *Foldrajzi Ertesito* 5, 71–80 (in Hungarian).

Tekse, K. 1965: Describing the geographical distribution of the population. *International Statistical Institute Review* 33, 259–69.

Thomas, C. 1985: Anton Melik 1890–1966. *Geographers' Bio-Bibliographical Studies* 9, 87–94.

Thomas, C. 1987: Svetozar Ilesic, 1907–1985. *Geographers' Bio-Bibliographical Studies*, 53–62.

Tkachenko, A. A. 1982: Sotsyologizatsya geografii i struktura ekonomiko-geograficheskoy nauki (The sociologisation of geography and the structure of economic geography). In *Voprosy sotsyalno-ekonomicheskoy geografii Verchnevolza*, Kalinin: Izdatelstvo Kalingradskogo Universiteta, 19–30.

Turnock, D. 1984: Vintila Mihailescu, 1890–1978. *Geographers' Bio-Bibliographical Studies* 61–7.

Turnock, D. 1988: Ion Conea, 1902–1974. *Geographers' Bio-Bibliographical Studies* 59–72.

Turska, A. 1989: Kreatywne i destruktywne czynniki aktywnosci grup lokalnych (The creative and destructive factors of the social activity of local groups). *Rozwoj Regionalny-Rozwoj Lokalny-Samorzad Terytorialny* 20, 102–18.

Turska, A. 1989: Wzory dzialan zbiorowych spolecznosci lokalnych z perspektywy ladu autorytarnego i demokratycznego *Rozwoj Regionalny-Rozwoj Lokalny-Samorzad Terytorialny* 27, 199–241.

Udaltsova, M. V. 1981: Teritorialnye obsledovania byudzheta vremeni (Territorial studies of the time budget). In Artemov, A. V. (ed.), *Obsledovania byudzheta vremeni zhiteley goroda i sela*, Novosibirsk: Nauka, 38–53.

Vabar, M. 1981: Obshchestvenno-geograficheskaya sistematika i razvitie geosfery (Socio-geographical systematics and the development of the geosphere). *Uchenye zapiski Tartuskogo Universiteta* 578, 6–24.

Valskaya, B. A. 1965: Veniamin Petrovich Semenov-Tyan-Shanski (1870–1942). In Baranski, N. N. (ed.), *Ekonomicheska geografia v SSSR*, Izd-vo Prosveshchenie, 398–432.

Vanagas, Y. 1987: Identifikatsya naselenia s zhiloy sredoy (Identification of people with a housing environment). In Yonaytis, V. (ed.), *Gorod: voprosy sotsyalnogo razvitia*, Vilnius: Institut Filosofii, Sotsyologii i Prava, 61–71.

Vasovic, M. 1980: Jovan Cvijic, 1865–1927. *Geographers' Bio-Bibliographical Studies* 25–32.

Velchev, I. 1967: The territorial and structural changes in Bulgaria's rural population in 1946–1965. *Izvestia na Bulgarsko Geografsko Druzestvo* 7, 109–26.

Veshninski, Y. G. 1983: O 'kriviznie' gorodskogo, sotsyalnogo prostranstva (About a 'curvature' of the urban social space). In Niit, T., Heidmets, M. and Kruusvall, J., *Psikhologia i arkhitektura*, Tallin: Tallinskiy Pedagogicheski Institut, 51–7.

Veshninski, Y. G. 1984: Sotsyalno-ekologicheskie aspekty vospriatia i otsenki prostranstvennoy sredy goroda (Socio-ecological aspects of perception and evaluation of the urban spatial environment). *Problemy biosfery* 6, 104–18.

Veshninski, Y. G. 1988: Sotsyalno-esteticheskie predpochtenia Moskvichey (Socio-aesthetic preferences of inhabitants of Moscow). In *Sotsyalnye problemy arkhitekturnogo i gradostroitelnogo razvitia Moskvy*, Moscow: Gorodizdat, 81–103.

Vlcek, I. 1964: Transportation links between rural settlements and service centres. *Zbornik Ceskoslovenske Spolecnosti Zemepisne* 69, 200–12 (in Czech).

Wakar, W. 1928: Podzial Polski na regiony przemyslowe (The division of

Poland into industrial regions). *Ekonomista*, 77–107.

Wallis, A. 1979: *Informacja i gwar. O miejskim centrum Warszawy* (Information and noise. About the city centre of Warsaw). Warsaw: Panstwowy Instytut Wydawniczy.

Wieruszewska, M. 1987: Wlasna wies w doswiadczeniu rolnikow indywidualnych (The village in the experience of peasants). *Rozwoj Regionalny-Rozwoj Lokalny-Samorzad Terytorialny* 6, 172–202.

Wieruszewska, M. 1989: Tozsamosc kulturowa jako wartosc i czynnik konstytuwny spolecznosci lokalnej (Cultural identity as a value and constitutive factor of local community). *Rozwoj Regionalny-Rozwoj Lokalny-Samorzad Terytorialny* 20, 302–24.

Witthauer, K. 1967: Zur sozialokonomischen Interpretation der Geburtenraten in der Sovjetunion. *Petermans Geographische Mitteilungen* 111, 237–9.

Wodz, J. 1989: Poczucie przynaleznosci lokalnej – niektore czynniki konstytutywne (The feeling of local identity – some constitutive factors). *Rozwoj Regionalny-Rozwoj Lokalny-Samorzad Terytorialny* 20, 44–60.

Wojtasiewicz, L. 1991: Wielkie regiony Polski na mapie Europy. Wielkopolska. Historia, terazniejszosc, przyszlosc (Large Polish regions on the map of Europe. Great Poland. The history, the present, the future). *Studia Regionalne i Lokalne* 1 (34), 33–84.

Wrobel, A. 1960: The study of an economic regional structure. *Przeglad Geograficzny* 32, 127–32 (supplement).

Yevteeva, N. V. 1987: Kto i pochemu vozvrashchaetsa v selo? (Who and why returns to the country?) *Sotsyologicheskie lasledovania*, 2, 61–64.

Yoffa, L. E. 1965: Vasilj Nikitich Tatishchev. In: Baranski N. N. (ed.), Ekonomicheskaia geografia v SSSR. Moscow: *Prosveshchenie*, 249–57.

Yugai, Y. L. 1985: Petr Ivanovich Rychkov, 1712–1777. *Geographers' Bio-Bibliographical Studies* 109–12.

Zaborski, B. 1926: O ksztaltach wsi w Polsce i ich rozmieszczeniu (About forms of villages in Poland and their distribution). *Prace Komisjii Etnograf.* PAU 1. Cracow.

Zaborski, B. 1964: Criteria for comparing settlement types. *Abstracts of Papers of the 20th International Geographical Congress.* London: Thomas Nelson and Sons, 316–17.

Zachariev, J. 1928: Kjustendilskoto kraisce (Kjustendilskoto region). *Sb. nar. um.*, 32, 3–102.

Zagozdzon, A. 1964: Zagadnienie ukladow osadniczych (Problems of settlement complexes). *Czasopismo Geograficzne* 35, 378–90.

Zaslavskaya, T. K. 1987: Rol sotsyologii v uskoreniu razvitia Sovetskogo obshchestva (The role of sociology in accelerating the development of Soviet society). *Sotsyologicheskie issledovania* 2, 3–15.

Zeranska-Kominek, S. 1989: Tradycja muzyczna jako czynnik nowej integracji spolecznej Litwinow w Polsce (Musical tradition as the factor of a new social integration of Lithuanians in Poland). *Rozwoj Regionalny-Rozwoj Lokalny-Samorzad Terytorialny*, 20, 343–61.

Znaniecki, F. 1931: *Miasto w swiadomosci jego obywateli*. Poznan: Polski Instytut Socjologiczny.

Znaniecki, F. 1938: Socjologiczne podstawy ekologii ludzkiej (Sociological foundations of human ecology). *Ruch Prawniczy, Ekonomiczny i Socjologiczny* 89.

Index